D1176473

THE YALE SHAKESPEARE

Revised Edition

General Editors

Helge Kökeritz and Charles T. Prouty

Published on the fund

given to the Yale University Press in 1917

by the members of the

Kingsley Trust Association

(Scroll and Key Society of Yale College)

to commemorate the seventy-fifth anniversary

of the founding of the society

THE YALE SHAKESPEARE

THE TAMING OF THE SHREW

Edited by Thomas G. Bergin

NEW HAVEN : YALE UNIVERSITY PRESS

London: Oxford University Press

FIRST PUBLISHED, MAY 1921
REVISED EDITION, MARCH 1954

Preface of the General Editors

AS the late Professor Tucker Brooke has observed, practically all modern editions of Shakespeare are 18th-century versions of the plays, based on the additions, alterations, and emendations of editors of that period. It has been our purpose, as it was Professor Brooke's, to give the modern reader Shakespeare's plays in the approximate form of their original appearance.

About half the plays appeared in quarto form before the publication of the First Folio in 1623. Thus for a large number of plays the only available text is that of the Folio. In the case of quarto plays our policy has been to use that text as the basis of the edition, unless it is clear that the text has been contaminated.

Interesting for us today is the fact that there are no act or scene divisions in the Quartos with the exception of *Othello*, which does mark Acts I, II, IV, and V but lacks indications of scenes. Even in the Folio, although act divisions are generally noted, only a part of the scenes are divided. In no case, either in Quarto or Folio, is there any indication of the place of action. The manifold scene divisions for the battle in such a play as *Antony and Cleopatra*, together with such locations as "Another part of the field," are the additions of the 18th century.

We have eliminated all indications of the place and time of action, because there is no authority for them in the originals and because Shakespeare gives such information, when it is requisite for understanding the play, through the dialogue of the actors. We have been sparing in our use of added scene and, in some cases, act divisions, because these frequently impede the flow of the action, which in Shakespeare's time was curiously like that of modern films.

Spelling has been modernized except when the original clearly indicates a pronunciation unlike our own, e.g. *desart* (desert), *divel* (devil), *banket* (banquet), and often in such Elizabethan syncopations as *stolne* (stol'n), and *tane* (ta'en). In reproducing such forms we have followed the inconsistent usage of the original.

We have also preserved the original capitalization when this is a part of the meaning. In like manner we have tended to adopt the lineation of the original in many cases where modern editors print prose as verse or verse as prose. We have, moreover, followed the original punctuation wherever it was practicable.

In verse we print a final *-ed* to indicate its full syllabic value, otherwise *'d*. In prose we have followed the inconsistencies of the original in this respect.

Our general practice has been to include in footnotes all information a reader needs for immediate understanding of the given page. In somewhat empiric fashion we repeat glosses as we think the reader needs to be reminded of the meaning. Further information is given in notes (indicated by the letter *N* in the footnotes) to be found at the back of each volume. Appendices deal with the text and sources of the play.

Square brackets indicate material not found in the original text. Long emendations or lines taken from another authoritative text of a play are indicated in the footnotes for the information of the reader. We have silently corrected obvious typographical errors.

CONTENTS

[THE ACTORS' NAMES

A LORD
CHRISTOPHER SLY, a tinker }
Hostess, Page, Players, Hunts- } persons in Act I,
   men, and Servants } Scene 1
BAPTISTA, a rich gentleman of Padua
VINCENTIO, an old gentleman of Pisa
LUCENTIO, son to Vincentio; in love with Bianca
PETRUCHIO, a gentleman of Verona; suitor to Kath-
   erina
GREMIO }
HORTENSIO } suitors to Bianca
TRANIO }
BIONDELLO } servants to Lucentio
GRUMIO }
CURTIS }
NATHANIEL }
PHILIP } servants to Petruchio
JOSEPH }
NICHOLAS }
PETER }
Pedant, set up to personate Vincentio
KATHERINA, the Shrew }
BIANCA } daughters to Baptista
Widow
Tailor, Haberdasher, and Servants

SCENE: *Padua, and Petruchio's house in the country*]

Act I

SCENE 1

Enter Beggar [Christopher Sly] and Hostess.

Sly. I'll pheeze you, in faith.

Hostess. A pair of stocks, you rogue!

Sly. Y'are a baggage: the Slys are no rogues; look in the chronicles; we came in with Richard Conqueror. Therefore, *paucas pallabris*; let the world slide. Sessa!   6

Hostess. You will not pay for the glasses you have burst?

Sly. No, not a denier. Go, by St. Jeronimy, go to thy cold bed and warm thee.   10

Hostess. I know my remedy: I must go fetch the third-borough.   [*Exit.*]

Sly. Third or fourth or fifth borough, I'll answer him by law. I'll not budge an inch, boy: let him come and kindly.   15

Falls asleep.

ACT 1, Scene 1 N. (N refers throughout to the corresponding note given at the end of the text.) SD ENTER ... HOSTESS (SD is used throughout to indicate stage directions.) F *Enter Begger and Hostess, Christopher Sly.* **1 Sly** F *Begger* throughout N. **pheeze you** do for you. **2 stocks** The hostess threatens Sly with being put in the stocks. **4 Richard** Sly's error for 'William.' **5 paucas pallabris** few words (corrupt Spanish). **6 Sessa** be quiet (French *cessez*). **9 denier** small copper coin, 'tenth of an English pennie.' **9 St. Jeronimy** N. **12 third-borough** constable; F *Head-borough.*

Wind horns. Enter a Lord from hunting, with his train.

Lord. Huntsman, I charge thee, tender well my
    hounds:
Broach Merriman, the poor cur is emboss'd,
And couple Clowder with the deep-mouth'd brach.
Saw'st thou not, boy, how Silver made it good
At the hedge-corner in the coldest fault?   20
I would not lose the dog for twenty pound.
  1. Huntsman. Why Bellman is as good as he, my
    lord;
He cried upon it at the merest loss
And twice today pick'd out the dullest scent.
Trust me, I take him for the better dog.   25
  Lord. Thou art a fool: if Echo were as fleet,
I would esteem him worth a dozen such.
But sup them well and look unto them all.
Tomorrow I intend to hunt again.
  1. Huntsman. I will, my lord.   30
  Lord. What's here? one dead or drunk? See, doth
    he breathe?
  2. Huntsman. He breathes, my lord. Were he not
    warm'd with ale
This were a bed but cold to sleep so soundly.
  Lord. O monstrous beast! how like a swine he lies!
Grim death, how foul and loathsome is thine image!
Sirs, I will practice on this drunken man.   36
What think you, if he were convey'd to bed,

---

16 **tender well** take good care of. 17 **Broach** F *Brach* N. **emboss'd**
foaming at the mouth from hard running. 18 **couple** N. **brach**
bitch. 20 **in the coldest fault** where the scent was nearly lost.
23 **cried upon it** gave tongue. **merest loss** when it was quite lost.
36 **practice** play a trick.

Wrapp'd in sweet clothes, rings put upon his fingers,
A most delicious banquet by his bed,
And brave attendants near him when he wakes,   40
Would not the beggar then forget himself?
  1. Huntsman. Believe me, lord, I think he cannot
    choose.
  2. Huntsman. It would seem strange unto him when
    he wak'd.
  Lord. Even as a flatt'ring dream or worthless fancy.
Then take him up and manage well the jest.   45
Carry him gently to my fairest chamber
And hang it round with all my wanton pictures,
Balm his foul head in warm distilled waters
And burn sweet wood to make the lodging sweet.
Procure me music ready when he wakes   50
To make a dulcet and a heavenly sound;
And if he chance to speak be ready straight,
And with a low submissive reverence
Say, 'What is it your honor will command?'
Let one attend him with a silver basin   55
Full of rose water and bestrew'd with flowers;
Another bear the ewer, the third a diaper,
And say, 'Will't please your lordship cool your
    hands?'
Some one be ready with a costly suit
And ask him what apparel he will wear,   60
Another tell him of his hounds and horse
And that his lady mourns at his disease.
Persuade him that he hath been lunatic;
And when he says he is, say that he dreams,
For he is nothing but a mighty lord.   65

40 **brave** finely dressed. 44 **even** read 'e'en.' 48 **Balm** perfume.
52 **straight** at once. 57 diaper towel. 64 **when he says he is** i.e.
when Sly says he is now mad.

This do, and do it kindly, gentle sirs.
It will be pastime passing excellent,
If it be husbanded with modesty.

  1. Huntsman. My lord, I warrant you we will play
    our part,
As he shall think, by our true diligence,   70
He is no less than what we say he is.

  Lord. Take him up gently, and to bed with him,
And each one to his office when he wakes.

             [Sly is borne out.] Sound trumpets.
Sirrah, go see what trumpet 'tis that sounds:
                  [Exit Servingman.]
Belike some noble gentleman that means,   75
Traveling some journey, to repose him here.

           Enter Servingman.

How now! who is it?
  Servingman.   An't please your honor, players
That offer service to your lordship.

            Enter Players.

  Lord. Bid them come near.
             Now, fellows, you are welcome.
  Players. We thank your honor.   80
  Lord. Do you intend to stay with me tonight?
  A Player. So please your lordship to accept our
    duty.
  Lord. With all my heart. This fellow I remember
Since once he play'd a farmer's eldest son:
'Twas where you woo'd the gentlewoman so well.   85

66 **kindly** naturally. 67 **passing** surpassingly. 68 **husbanded** managed. **modesty** moderation. 69 **warrant** read 'warn't'. 70 **As** so that. 75 **Belike** probably. 77 **An't** if it. SD **Enter Players** N. 79 **come near** enter. 82 **A Player** F *Player.* **duty** expression of respect.

  4

I have forgot your name; but sure that part
Was aptly fitted and naturally perform'd.
  A Player. I think 'twas Soto that your honor
      means.
  Lord. 'Tis very true: thou didst it excellent.
Well, you are come to me in happy time,   90
The rather for I have some sport in hand
Wherein your cunning can assist me much.
There is a lord will hear you play tonight;
But I am doubtful of your modesties,
Lest, over-eyeing of his odd behavior—   95
For yet his honor never heard a play—
You break into some merry passion
And so offend him; for I tell you, sirs,
If you should smile he grows impatient.
  A Player. Fear not, my lord, we can contain our-
      selves   100
Were he the veriest antic in the world.
  Lord. Go, sirrah, take them to the buttery
And give them friendly welcome every one.
Let them want nothing that my house affords.
                              Exit one with the Players.
Sirrah, go you to Barthol'mew my page   105
And see him dress'd in all suits like a lady:
That done, conduct him to the drunkard's chamber
And call him 'madam'; do him obeisance.
Tell him from me—as he will win my love—
He bear himself with honorable action   110

87 **naturally** read 'nat'rally.' 88 **A Player** F *Sincklo* N. **Soto** N.
91 **The rather for** the more so because. 92 **cunning** skill. 94
modesties discretion. 95 **over-eyeing** observing. 97 **merry passion**
fit of laughter. 101 **antic** eccentric. 102 **buttery** room where drink
is kept. 104 **want** lack. 105 **page** N. 106 **in all suits** in every
respect.

Such as he hath observ'd in noble ladies
Unto their lords, by them accomplished:
Such duty to the drunkard let him do
With soft low tongue and lowly courtesy,
And say, 'What is't your honor will command   115
Wherein your lady and your humble wife
May show her duty and make known her love?'
And then, with kind embracements, tempting kisses,
And with declining head into his bosom,
Bid him shed tears, as being overjoy'd   120
To see her noble lord restor'd to health
Who for this seven years hath esteemed him
No better than a poor and loathsome beggar.
And if the boy have not a woman's gift
To rain a shower of commanded tears   125
An onion will do well for such a shift,
Which in a napkin being close convey'd
Shall in despite enforce a watery eye.
See this dispatch'd with all the haste thou canst:
Anon I'll give thee more instructions.   130

Exit a Servingman.

I know the boy will well usurp the grace,
Voice, gait, and action of a gentlewoman.
I long to hear him call the drunkard husband,
And how my men will stay themselves from laughter
When they do homage to this simple peasant.   135
I'll in to counsel them: haply my presence
May well abate the over merry spleen

112 **them** pleonastic, referring to ladies. **accomplished** performed.
113 **duty** service. 122 **him** himself. 126 **shift** purpose. 127 **napkin**
handkerchief. **close** secretly. 128 **watery** read 'wat'ry.' 130 **anon**
presently. 131 **usurp** imitate. 134 **stay** keep. 137 **spleen** mood
(the spleen was thought to be the seat of passions).

Which otherwise would grow into extremes.

[*Exeunt.*]

[SCENE 2]

*Enter aloft the drunkard [Sly], with attendants,
some with apparel, [others with] basin and ewer,
and other appurtenances, and Lord.*

Sly. For God's sake! a pot of small ale.

1. Servingman. Will't please your lordship drink a
cup of sack?

2. Servingman. Will't please your honor taste of
these conserves?

3. Servingman. What raiment will your honor wear
today?   4

Sly. I am Christophero Sly; call not me honor nor
lordship. I ne'er drank sack in my life; and if you
give me any conserves, give me conserves of beef.
Ne'er ask me what raiment I'll wear for I have no
more doublets than backs, no more stockings than
legs nor no more shoes than feet: nay, sometime more
feet than shoes or such shoes as my toes look through
the overleather.   12

Lord. Heaven cease this idle humor in your honor!
O that a mighty man of such descent,
Of such possessions and so high esteem
Should be infused with so foul a spirit!   16

Sly. What! would you make me mad? Am not I
Christopher Sly, old Sly's son, of Burton-heath; by

SD **aloft** i.e. on the balcony at the back of the stage. **ewer** wide-
mouthed pitcher. 2 **sack** Spanish and Canary wine. 7 **conserves
of beef** salt beef. 13 **idle humor** absurd fancy. 18 **Sly's** F. *Sies.*
Burton-heath perhaps Barton-on-the-Heath, a Warwickshire
village.

birth a pedlar, by education a cardmaker, by trans-
mutation a bearherd, and now by present profession
a tinker? Ask Marian Hacket, the fat ale-wife of
Wincot, if she know me not: if she say I am not
fourteen pence on the score for sheer ale score me
up for the lyingest knave in Christendom. What! I
am not bestraught: here's—   25

    3. Servingman. O! this it is that makes your lady
      mourn.

    2. Servingman. O! this is it that makes your serv-
      ants droop.

    Lord. Hence comes it that your kindred shuns your
      house

As beaten hence by your strange lunacy.
O noble lord, bethink thee of thy birth,   30
Call home thy ancient thoughts from banishment
And banish hence these abject lowly dreams.
Look how thy servants do attend on thee,
Each in his office ready at thy beck.   34
Wilt thou have music? hark! Apollo plays,   *Music.*
And twenty caged nightingales do sing.
Or wilt thou sleep? we'll have thee to a couch
Softer and sweeter than the lustful bed
On purpose trimm'd up for Semiramis.
Say thou wilt walk, we will bestrow the ground;   40
Or wilt thou ride? thy horses shall be trapp'd,
Their harness studded all with gold and pearl.
Dost thou love hawking? thou hast hawks will soar

19 **cardmaker** cards are instruments for combing wool. 20 **bearherd** one who leads about a tame bear. 22 **Wincot** a place, once
a hamlet, near Stratford. 23 **sheer ale** i.e. ale only. 25 **bestraught**
Sly means 'distraught.' 26 **3. Servingman** F *3 Man.* 31 **ancient
thoughts** former reason. 35 **Apollo** god of music. 39 **Semiramis**
legendary lustful queen of Assyria. 41 **trapp'd** adorned. 43 **will
soar** which will soar.

Above the morning lark; or wilt thou hunt?
Thy hounds shall make the welkin answer them   45
And fetch shrill echoes from the hollow earth.

   1. Servingman. Say thou wilt course, thy grey-
      hounds are as swift
As breathed stags, ay, fleeter than the roe.

   2. Servingman. Dost thou love pictures? we will
      fetch thee straight
Adonis painted by a running brook   50
And Cytherea all in sedges hid,
Which seem to move and wanton with her breath
Even as the waving sedges play with wind.

   Lord. We'll show thee Io as she was a maid
And how she was beguiled and surpris'd   55
As lively painted as the deed was done.

   3. Servingman. Or Daphne roaming through a
      thorny wood,
Scratching her legs that one shall swear she bleeds;
And at that sight shall sad Apollo weep,
So workmanly the blood and tears are drawn.   60

   Lord. Thou art a lord and nothing but a lord;
Thou hast a lady far more beautiful
Than any woman in this waning age.

   1. Servingman. And till the tears that she hath
      shed for thee
Like envious floods o'errun her lovely face   65
She was the fairest creature in the world,
And yet she is inferior to none.

   Sly. Am I a lord? and have I such a lady?
Or do I dream? or have I dream'd till now?

45 **welkin** sky. 47 **course** hunt hares with greyhounds. 48 **breathed**
in full breath. **roe** a type of small deer. 50 **Adonis** N. 51 **Cytherea**
Venus. 52 **wanton** sway lasciviously. 53 **even** read 'e'en.' 54 **Io**
Greek maiden loved by Zeus. 57 **Daphne** N. 60 **workmanly** skill-
fully. 63 **waning** degenerate.

I do not sleep; I see, I hear, I speak;   70
I smell sweet savors and I feel soft things:
Upon my life, I am a lord indeed
And not a tinker nor Christopher Sly.
Well, bring our lady hither to our sight
And once again, a pot o' th' smallest ale.   75
  2. Servingman. Will't please your mightiness to
    wash your hands?
O, how we joy to see your wit restor'd!
O, that once more you knew but what you are!
These fifteen years you have bin in a dream,
Or when you wak'd so wak'd as if you slept.   80
  Sly. These fifteen years! by my fay, a goodly nap.
But did I never speak of all that time?
  1. Servingman. O yes, my lord, but very idle words;
For though you lay here in this goodly chamber,
Yet would you say ye were beaten out of door   85
And rail upon the hostess of the house
And say you would present her at the leet
Because she brought stone jugs and no seal'd quarts.
Sometimes you would call out for Cicely Hacket.
  Sly. Ay, the woman's maid of the house.   90
  3. Servingman. Why, sir, you know no house nor
    no such maid
Nor no such men as you have reckon'd up,
As Stephen Sly, and old John Naps of Greece,
And Peter Turf, and Henry Pimpernell,
And twenty more such names and men as these   95
Which never were nor no man ever saw.

---

75 **smallest** weakest. 77 **wit** reason. 81 **by my** read 'bim.' **fay** faith.
82 **of** in. 87 **leet** manorial court where, among others, those ac-
cused of using false measures were tried. 88 **seal'd** stamped with
official seal indicating capacity. 89 **Cicely** read 'Cic'ly.' 93–4 **As
Stephen Sly . . . Henry Pimpernell** N.

Sly. Now, Lord be thanked for my good amends!
All. Amen.

Enter [the Page, as a] Lady, with Attendants.

Sly. I thank thee; thou shalt not lose by it.
Page. How fares my noble lord? 100
Sly. Marry, I fare well for here is cheer enough.
Where is my wife?
Page. Here, noble lord: what is thy will with her?
Sly. Are you my wife and will not call me husband?
My men should call me lord: I am your goodman.
Page. My husband and my lord, my lord and hus-
band; 106
I am your wife in all obedience.
Sly. I know it well. What must I call her?
Lord. Madam.
Sly. Al'ce madam or Joan madam? 110
Lord. Madam and nothing else: so lords call ladies.
Sly. Madam wife, they say that I have dream'd
And slept above some fifteen year or more.
Page. Ay, and the time seems thirty unto me,
Being all this time abandon'd from your bed. 115
Sly. 'Tis much. Servants, leave me and her alone.
Madam, undress you and come now to bed.
Page. Thrice noble lord, let me entreat of you
To pardon me yet for a night or two,
Or, if not so, until the sun be set: 120
For your physicians have expressly charg'd,
In peril to incur your former malady,
That I should yet absent me from your bed.
I hope this reason stands for my excuse. 124

97 **amends** recovery. SD **Page, as a Lady** F *Lady* throughout.
115 **abandon'd** banished. 122 **to incur** of incurring. 124 **reason**
pronounced 'raisin,' allowing play on 'raising.'

Sly. Ay, it stands so, that I may hardly tarry so long; but I would be loath to fall into my dreams again: I will therefore tarry in despite of the flesh and the blood.

Enter a Messenger.

Messenger. Your honor's players, hearing your amendment,
Are come to play a pleasant comedy;   130
For so your doctors hold it very meet,
Seeing too much sadness hath congeal'd your blood,
And melancholy is the nurse of frenzy:
Therefore they thought it good you hear a play
And frame your mind to mirth and merriment,   135
Which bars a thousand harms and lengthens life.
Sly. Marry, I will let them play. It is not a comonty, a Christmas gambold, or a tumbling-trick?
Page. No, my good lord, it is more pleasing stuff.
Sly. What! household stuff?   140
Page. It is a kind of history.
Sly. Well, we'll see't. Come, madam wife, sit by my side
And let the world slip: we shall nere be younger.
Flourish.

[SCENE 3]

Enter Lucentio and his man Tranio.

Lucentio. Tranio, since for the great desire I had
To see fair Padua, nursery of arts,

137–8 **comonty** Sly's version of 'comedy.' **gambold** gambol, 'stunt.' 143 **nere** never. SD **Flourish** meaning 'sound the trumpets.' 2–3 **Padua . . . Lumbardy** N.

I am arriv'd for fruitful Lumbardy,
The pleasant garden of great Italy,
And by my father's love and leave am arm'd   5
With his good will and thy good company,
My trusty servant well approv'd in all,
Here let us breathe and haply institute
A course of learning and ingenious studies.
Pisa, renowned for grave citizens,   10
Gave me my being and my father first,
A merchant of great traffic through the world,
Vincentio come of the Bentivolii.
Vincentio's son, brought up in Florence,
It shall become to serve all hopes conceiv'd,   15
To deck his fortune with his virtuous deeds:
And therefore, Tranio, for the time I study,
Virtue and that part of philosophy
Will I apply that treats of happiness
By virtue specially to be achiev'd.   20
Tell me thy mind, for I have Pisa left
And am to Padua come, as he that leaves
A shallow plash to plunge him in the deep
And with satiety seeks to quench his thirst.
    Tranio. Me pardonato, gentle master mine: 25
I am in all affected as yourself,
Glad that you thus continue your resolve
To suck the sweets of sweet philosophy.
Only, good master, while we do admire
This virtue and this moral discipline,   30
Let's be no stoics nor no stocks, I pray;
Or so devote to Aristotle's checks

3 for in. 7 approv'd tried. 8 institute begin. 9 ingenious intel-
lectual. 15 serve fulfill. 19 apply study. 23 plash pool. 25 Me
pardonato begging your pardon (bad Italian). 26 affected
disposed. 31 stocks wooden creatures, like posts—with play
on 'stoics.' 32 devote devoted. checks restraints.

As Ovid be an outcast quite abjur'd.
Balk logic with acquaintance that you have
And practice rhetoric in your common talk.   35
Music and poesy use to quicken you;
The mathematics and the metaphysics,
Fall to them as you find your stomach serves you.
No profit grows where is no pleasure tane;
In brief, sir, study what you most affect.   40
   Lucentio. Gramercies, Tranio, well dost thou advise.
If, Biondello, thou wert come ashore,
We could at once put us in readiness
And take a lodging fit to entertain
Such friends as time in Padua shall beget.   45
But stay awhile: what company is this?
   Tranio. Master, some show to welcome us to town.

*Enter Baptista with his two daughters, Katherina
and Bianca, Gremio, a Pantaloon, [and] Hortensio,
suitor to Bianca. Lucentio [and] Tranio stand by.*

   Baptista. Gentlemen, importune me no farther,
For how I firmly am resolv'd you know;
That is, not to bestow my youngest daughter   50
Before I have a husband for the elder.
If either of you both love Katherina,
Because I know you well and love you well,
Leave shall you have to court her at your pleasure.
   Gremio. To cart her rather; she's too rough for me.
There, there, Hortensio, will you any wife?   56
   Katherina. I pray you, sir, is it your will

33 **As** so that. **Ovid** the poet of love. 34 **Balk logic** bandy argu-
ments, use dialectic. 36 **poesy** monosyllabic here. **quicken** stimu-
late. 37 **metaphysics** N. 38 **stomach** inclination. 39 **tane** taken.
40 **affect** care for. 41 **Gramercies** many thanks. SD **Pantaloon** N.
Katherina F *Katerina*, and so pronounced. **suitor** F *sister*. **by**
aside. 55 **cart** N.

To make a stale of me amongst these mates?

  Hortensio. Mates, maid! how mean you that? no
    mates for you

Unless you were of gentler, milder mold.   60

  Katherina. I' faith, sir, you shall never need to
    fear:

Iwis it is not halfway to her heart;

But if it were, doubt not her care should be

To comb your noddle with a three-legg'd stool

And paint your face and use you like a fool.   65

  Hortensio. From all such divels, good Lord deliver
    us!

  Gremio. And me too, good Lord!

  Tranio. Husht, master! here is some good pastime
    toward.

That wench is stark mad or wonderful froward.

  Lucentio. But in the other's silence do I see   70

Maid's mild behavior and sobriety.

Peace, Tranio!

  Tranio. Well said, master; mum! and gaze your fill.

  Baptista. Gentlemen, that I may soon make good

What I have said—Bianca, get you in: 75

And let it not displease thee, good Bianca,

For I will love thee nere the less, my girl.

  Katherina. A pretty pet! it is best

Put finger in the eye, an she knew why.

  Bianca. Sister, content you in my discontent.   80

Sir, to your pleasure humbly I subscribe:

My books and instruments shall be my company,

---

58 **stale** laughingstock. **mates** (low) fellows, with pun on 'stale-
mate,' chess term. 59 **mates** husbands. 62 **Iwis** indeed. 65 **paint
your face** i.e. with scratches. 68 **toward** at hand. 69 **froward** bold.
73 **master** F *Mr.* 78-9 **it is best . . . knew why** let her cry—if
she only knew what cause she has.

On them to look and practice by myself.

   Lucentio. Hark, Tranio! thou mayst hear Minerva
     speak.   84

   Hortensio. Signior Baptista, will you be so strange?
Sorry am I that our good will effects
Bianca's grief.

   Gremio.   Why will you mew her up,
Signior Baptista, for this fiend of hell
And make her bear the penance of her tongue?

   Baptista. Gentlemen, content ye; I am resolv'd.   90
Go in, Bianca.   [*Exit Bianca.*]
And for I know she taketh most delight
In music, instruments, and poetry,
Schoolmasters will I keep within my house,
Fit to instruct her youth. If you, Hortensio,   95
Or Signior Gremio, you, know any such,
Prefer them hither; for to cunning men
I will be very kind, and liberal
To mine own children in good bringing up;
And so, farewell. Katherina, you may stay   100
For I have more to commune with Bianca.   *Exit.*

   Katherina. Why, and I trust I may go too; may I
     not?
What! shall I be appointed hours, as though, belike,
I knew not what to take and what to leave? Ha!
                                   Exit.

   Gremio. You may go to the divel's dam: your gifts
are so good, here's none will hold you. Their love is

84 **Minerva** goddess of wisdom. 85 **strange** unkind (to Bianca).
87 **mew** shut, a term from falconry. 92 **for** since. 97 **prefer** recommend. **cunning** well-trained, able. 105 **to the divel's dam** to the
devil. **gifts** endowments. 106–107 **Their love is not so great** The
love of women is not so important N.

16

not so great, Hortensio, but we may blow our nails together and fast it fairly out; our cake's dough on both sides. Farewell: yet, for the love I bear my sweet Bianca, if I can by any means light on a fit man to teach her that wherein she delights, I will wish him to her father.   112

Hortensio. So will I, Signor Gremio: but a word, I pray. Though the nature of our quarrel yet never brooked parle, know now, upon advice, it toucheth us both—that we may yet again have access to our fair mistress and be happy rivals in Bianca's love—to labor and effect one thing specially.

Gremio. What's that, I pray?   119

Hortensio. Marry, sir, to get a husband for her sister.

Gremio. A husband! a divel.

Hortensio. I say, a husband.

Gremio. I say, a divel. Thinkst thou, Hortensio, though her father be very rich, any man is so very a fool to be married to hell?   126

Hortensio. Tush, Gremio! though it pass your patience and mine to endure her loud alarums, why, man, there be good fellows in the world, an a man could light on them, would take her with all faults, and money enough.   131

Gremio. I cannot tell; but I had as lief take her dowry with this condition, to be whipped at the high-cross every morning.   134

Hortensio. Faith, as you say, there's small choice in rotten apples. But come; since this bar in law makes

107–108 **blow our nails together** be patient. **fairly** well. 108–109 **our cake's . . . sides** our goose is cooked. 111 **wish** recommend. 115 **brooked parle** permitted negotiation. **advice** reflection. 126 **to be** as to be. 129 **be** are (old plural). 133–4 **high-cross** cross in the central square or market of a town.

us friends, it shall be so far forth friendly main-
tained, till by helping Baptista's eldest daughter to
a husband, we set his youngest free for a husband,
and then have to't afresh. Sweet Bianca! Happy man
be his dole! He that runs fastest gets the ring. How
say you, Signior Gremio?   142

Gremio. I am agreed: and would I had given him
the best horse in Padua to begin his wooing, that
would thoroughly woo her, wed her, and bed her, and
rid the house of her. Come on.   146

    Exeunt ambo. Mane[n]t Tranio and Lucentio.

Tranio. I pray, sir, tell me, is it possible
That love should of a sudden take such hold?

Lucentio. O Tranio! till I found it to be true
I never thought it possible or likely.   150
But see, while idly I stood looking on,
I found the effect of love in idleness
And now in plainness do confess to thee,
That art to me as secret and as dear
As Anna to the Queen of Carthage was,   155
Tranio, I burn, I pine, I perish, Tranio,
If I achieve not this young modest girl.
Counsel me, Tranio, for I know thou canst.
Assist me, Tranio, for I know thou wilt.

Tranio. Master, it is no time to chide you now;   160
Affection is not rated from the heart:
If love have touch'd you, nought remains but so,
Redime te captam, quam queas minimo.

Lucentio. Gramercies, lad; go forward. This con-
    tents;

140 **have to't afresh** resume our rivalry. 140–41 **Happy man be his dole** may his lot be that of a happy man. **SD ambo** both (Gremio and Hortensio). **Mane[n]t** remain. 152 **the effect** read 'th'effect.' **love in idleness** N. 155 **Anna** N. 161 **rated** driven out by scolding. 163 **Redime . . . minimo** N. 164 **Gramercies** many thanks.

18

The rest will comfort, for thy counsel's sound.   165

Tranio. Master, you look'd so longly on the maid,
Perhaps you mark'd not what's the pith of all.

Lucentio. O yes, I saw sweet beauty in her face,
Such as the daughter of Agenor had,   169
That made great Jove to humble him to her hand
When with his knees he kiss'd the Cretan strond.

Tranio. Saw you no more? mark'd you not how her
     sister
Began to scold and raise up such a storm
That mortal ears might hardly endure the din?

Lucentio. Tranio, I saw her coral lips to move   175
And with her breath she did perfume the air.
Sacred and sweet was all I saw in her.

Tranio. Nay, then, 'tis time to stir him from his
     trance.
I pray, awake, sir: if you love the maid
Bend thoughts and wits to achieve her. Thus it
     stands: 180
Her elder sister is so curst and shrewd
That till the father rid his hands of her,
Master, your love must live a maid at home;
And therefore has he closely mew'd her up,
Because she will not be annoy'd with suitors.   185

Lucentio. Ah, Tranio, what a cruel father's he!
But art thou not advis'd he took some care
To get her cunning schoolmasters to instruct her?

Tranio. Ay, marry, am I, sir; and now 'tis plotted.

Lucentio. I have it, Tranio.

Tranio.   Master, for my hand,

166 **longly** longingly or persistently. 167 **pith** essential point. 169
daughter of Agenor N. 171 **strond** strand. 180 **to achieve** read
't'achieve' (cf. l. 220). 181 **curst** bad tempered. **shrewd** shrewish.
185 **Because she will not** so that she may not. 187 **advis'd** aware.
190 **for** I'll bet.

Both our inventions meet and jump in one.   191

  Lucentio. Tell me thine first.

  Tranio.   You will be school-master

And undertake the teaching of the maid;

That's your device.

  Lucentio.   It is; may it be done?

  Tranio. Not possible, for who shall bear your part

And be in Padua here Vincentio's son?   196

Keep house and ply his book, welcome his friends,

Visit his countrymen and banquet them?

  Lucentio. *Basta*, content thee; for I have it full.

We have not yet been seen in any house   200

Nor can we be distinguish'd by our faces

For man or master: then, it follows thus:

Thou shalt be master, Tranio, in my stead,

Keep house, and port, and servants, as I should.

I will some other be; some Florentine,   205

Some Neapolitan, or meaner man of Pisa.

'Tis hatch'd and shall be so: Tranio, at once

Uncase thee, take my color'd hat and cloak.

When Biondello comes he waits on thee;

But I will charm him first to keep his tongue.   210

  Tranio. So had you need.

In brief, sir, sith it your pleasure is

And I am tied to be obedient—

For so your father charg'd me at our parting;

'Be serviceable to my son,' quoth he,   215

Although I think 'twas in another sense—

I am content to be Lucentio

191 **jump** join. 194 **may** can. 199 **Basta** enough (Italian). **full** all planned. 204 **port** style of living. 206 **meaner** of lower class. 208 **Uncase thee** take off your coat. **color'd** Tranio, as becomes a servant, is wearing a sober costume; Lucentio is more gaily clad. 210 **charm** compel by enchantment. 212 **sith** since.

Because so well I love Lucentio.

Lucentio. Tranio, be so, because Lucentio loves,
And let me be a slave, t'achieve that maid   220
Whose sudden sight hath thrall'd my wounded eye.
Here comes the rogue.

Enter Biondello

                Sirrah, where have you bin?

Biondello. Where have I been! Nay, how now! where
    are you?
Master, has my fellow Tranio stolne your clothes,
Or you stolne his? or both? pray, what's the news?

Lucentio. Sirrah, come hither: 'tis no time to jest,
And therefore frame your manners to the time.
Your fellow Tranio, here, to save my life,
Puts my apparel and my count'nance on
And I for my escape have put on his;   230
For in a quarrel since I came ashore
I kill'd a man and fear I was descried.
Wait you on him, I charge you, as becomes,
While I make way from hence to save my life.
You understand me?

Biondello.   I, sir! nere a whit.   235

Lucentio. And not a jot of Tranio in your mouth.
Tranio is chang'd into Lucentio.

Biondello. The better for him: would I were so too!

Tranio. So could I, faith, boy, to have the next wish
    after,
That Lucentio indeed had Baptista's youngest
    daughter.   240

---

221 **thrall'd** enthralled. 222 **Sirrah** usual form of addressing servants. 224 **stolne** stolen. 229 **count'nance** outward appearance.
239–44 **So could I . . . your master,** Lucentio F sets as prose.

But, sirrah, not for my sake, but your master's, I
    advise
You use your manners discreetly in all kind of com-
    panies:
When I am alone, why, then I am Tranio;
But in all places else your master, Lucentio.
  Lucentio. Tranio, let's go.   245
One thing more rests, that thyself execute,
To make one among these wooers: if thou ask me
    why,
Sufficeth my reasons are both good and weighty.
                            Exeunt.

The Presenters above speak.

1. Servingman. My lord, you nod; you do not mind
the play.   249

Sly. Yes, by Saint Anne, I do. A good matter,
surely; comes there any more of it?

Page. My lord, 'tis but begun.

Sly. 'Tis a very excellent piece of work, madam
lady: would 'twere done!   *They sit and mark.*

[SCENE 4]

Enter Petruchio, and his man Grumio.

Petruchio. Verona, for awhile I take my leave
To see my friends in Padua; but, of all
My best beloved and approved friend,
Hortensio; and I trow this is his house.

---

246 rests remains. execute carry out. SD Presenters actors. speak
F *speakes.* 249 mind pay attention to. SD mark watch. 4 trow
believe.

Here, sirrah Grumio; knock, I say.   5

Grumio. Knock, sir? whom should I knock? is there
any man has rebused your worship?

Petruchio. Villain, I say, knock me here soundly.

Grumio. Knock you here, sir? why, sir, what am I,
sir, that I should knock you here, sir?   10

Petruchio. Villain, I say, knock me at this gate
And rap me well or I'll knock your knave's pate.

Grumio. My master is grown quarrelsome. I should
    knock you first
And then I know after who comes by the worst.

Petruchio. Will it not be?   15
Faith, sirrah, and you'll not knock, I'll rin it;
I'll try how you can *sol, fa,* and sing it.

                He wrings him by the ears.

Grumio. Help, masters, help! my master is mad.

Petruchio. Now, knock when I bid you, sirrah vil-
lain!   20

Enter Hortensio.

Hortensio. How now, what's the matter? My old
friend Grumio! and my good friend Petruchio! How
do you all at Verona?

Petruchio. Signior Hortensio, come you to part the
    fray?
Con tutto il cuore ben trovato, may I say.   25

---

7 **rebused** Grumio's version of 'abused.' 8 **me** i.e. 'for me' (the
ethical dative); Grumio willfully misunderstands *me here* as 'my
ear.' **soundly** vigorously. 12 **pate** head. 16 **and** if. **ring** with play
on 'wring'; see following SD. 17 **sol, fa** notes on the scale, said
to the accompaniment of the stage business. 18 **masters** F *mistris.*
25 **Con . . . trovato** with all my heart well met (literally, 'found');
F *Con tutti le core bene trobatto.*

23

Hortensio. Alla nostra casa ben venuto, molto honorato signior mio Petruchio.

Rise, Grumio, rise: we will compound this quarrel.

Grumio. Nay, 'tis no matter, sir, what he 'leges in Latin. If this be not a lawful cause for me to leave his service, look you, sir, he bid me knock him and rap him soundly, sir: well, was it fit for a servant to use his master so; being, perhaps, for aught I see, two-and-thirty, a peep out?

Whom would to God, I had well knock'd at first, 35
Then had not Grumio come by the worst.

Petruchio. A senseless villain! Good Hortensio,
I bade the rascal knock upon your gate
And could not get him for my heart to do it. 39

Grumio. Knock at the gate? O heavens! Spake you not these words plain, 'Sirrah, knock me here, rap me here, knock me well, and knock me soundly?' And come you now with 'knocking at the gate'?

Petruchio. Sirrah, be gone, or talk not, I advise you.

Hortensio. Petruchio, patience; I am Grumio's pledge. 45

Why, this a heavy chance 'twixt him and you,
Your ancient, trusty, pleasant servant Grumio.
And tell me now, sweet friend, what happy gale
Blows you to Padua here from old Verona?

26–7 **Alla . . . Petruchio** Welcome to our house, my most honored Signor Petruchio. **ben** F. *bene*. **molto** F *multo*. **honorato** F *honorata*. 28 **compound** settle. 29 **'leges** alleges. 30 **Latin** so the foregoing 'foreign talk' seems to Grumio. 34 **two-and-thirty, a peep out** expression derived from an old card game, meaning 'intoxicated.' **peep** pip, one of the suit markings on a playing card. 35–6 **Whom would . . . the worst** F sets as prose. 46 **this** this is. **heavy** sad.

24

Petruchio. Such wind as scatters young men
    through the world   50
To seek their fortunes farther than at home,
Where small experience grows. But in a few,
Signior Hortensio, thus it stands with me:
Antonio, my father, is deceas'd
And I have thrust myself into this maze,   55
Happily to wive and thrive as best I may.
Crowns in my purse I have and goods at home
And so am come abroad to see the world.

  Hortensio. Petruchio, shall I then come roundly to
    thee
And wish thee to a shrewd ill-favor'd wife?   60
Thou'dst thank me but a little for my counsel
And yet I'll promise thee she shall be rich,
And very rich: but thou'rt too much my friend
And I'll not wish thee to her.

  Petruchio. Signior Hortensio, 'twixt such friends as
    we   65
Few words suffice; and therefore, if thou know
One rich enough to be Petruchio's wife,
As wealth is burthen of my wooing dance,
Be she as foul as was Florentius' love,
As old as Sibyl, and as curst and shrowd   70
As Socrates' Zentippe, or a worse,
She moves me not, or not removes, at least,
Affection's edge in me, were she as rough
As are the swelling Adriatic seas.
I come to wive it wealthily in Padua;   75
If wealthily, then happily in Padua.

52 **in a few** i.e. words. 57 **crowns** coins. 59 **come roundly** speak
plainly. 68 **burthen** the accompaniment. 69 **foul** ugly. **Florentius'**
N. 70 **Sibyl** legendary female prophet N. **shrowd** shrewd. 71
Zentippe Xanthippe, Socrates' shrewish wife. 73 **as** F *is as.*

Grumio. Nay, look you, sir, he tells you flatly what his mind is; why, give him gold enough and marry him to a puppet or an aglet-baby or an old trot with ne'er a tooth in her head, though she have as many diseases as two-and-fifty horses: why, nothing comes amiss so money comes withal.   82

Hortensio. Petruchio, since we are stepp'd thus far in,
I will continue that I broach'd in jest.
I can, Petruchio, help thee to a wife   85
With wealth enough and young and beauteous,
Brought up as best becomes a gentlewoman.
Her only fault—and that is faults enough—
Is that she is intolerable curst   89
And shrowd and froward, so beyond all measure,
That were my state far worser than it is
I would not wed her for a mine of gold.

Petruchio. Hortensio, peace! thou know'st not gold's effect.
Tell me her father's name, and 'tis enough;
For I will board her though she chide as loud   95
As thunder when the clouds in autumn crack.

Hortensio. Her father is Baptista Minola,
An affable and courteous gentleman;
Her name is Katherina Minola,
Renown'd in Padua for her scolding tongue.   100

Petruchio. I know her father though I know not her,
And he knew my deceased father well.
I will not sleep, Hortensio, till I see her;

79 **aglet-baby** small figure carved on the tag of a point of lace (French *aiguillette*). **trot** hag. 84 **that** what. 89 **intolerable** intolerably. 90 **froward** contrary. 91 **state** financial condition. 95 **board** approach, woo. **chide** scold.

And therefore let me be thus bold with you,
To give you over at this first encounter   105
Unless you will accompany me thither.

  Grumio. I pray you, sir, let him go while the humor
lasts. A my word, and she knew him as well as I do
she would think scolding would do little good upon
him. She may perhaps call him half a score knaves
or so: why, that's nothing: and he begin once, he'll
rail in his rope-tricks. I'll tell you what, sir, an she
stand him but a little, he will throw a figure in her
face and so disfigure her with it that she shall have
no more eyes to see withal than a cat. You know him
not, sir.   116

  Hortensio. Tarry, Petruchio, I must go with thee
For in Baptista's keep my treasure is.
He hath the jewel of my life in hold,
His youngest daughter, beautiful Bianca,   120
And her withholds from me and other more,
Suitors to her and rivals in my love,
Supposing it a thing impossible,
For those defects I have before rehears'd,
That ever Katherina will be woo'd.   125
Therefore this order hath Baptista tane,
That none shall have access unto Bianca
Till Katherine the curst have got a husband.

  Grumio. Katherine the curst!
A title for a maid of all titles the worst.   130

---

105 give **you over** leave you. 108 **A** on. 112 **rope-tricks** tricks
worthy of the rope (i.e. hanging) with play on 'rhetorics'; cf.
figure, l. 113. 113 **stand** withstand. 115 **cat** perhaps because a cat
has eyes half closed in daytime, with incidental play on 'cat' and
'Kate.' 121 **me and other more** F *me. Other more.* 126 **order . . .
tane** measures . . . taken.

Hortensio. Now shall my friend Petruchio do me
    grace
And offer me, disguis'd in sober robes,
To old Baptista as a schoolmaster
Well seen in music, to instruct Bianca,
That so I may, by this device, at least   135
Have leave and leisure to make love to her
And unsuspected court her by herself.

Enter Gremio, and Lucentio disguised.

Grumio. Here's no knavery! See, to beguile the old
folks, how the young folks lay their heads together!
Master, master, look about you: who goes there, ha?
   Hortensio. Peace, Grumio! it is the rival of my love.
Petruchio, stand by awhile.   142
   Grumio. A proper stripling, and an amorous!
   Gremio. O! very well; I have perus'd the note.
Hark you, sir; I'll have them very fairly bound: 145
All books of love, see that at any hand,
And see you read no other lectures to her.
You understand me. Over and beside
Signior Baptista's liberality,
I'll mend it with a largess. Take your paper too 150
And let me have them very well perfum'd,
For she is sweeter than perfume itself
To whom they go to. What will you read to her?
   Lucentio. What ere I read to her, I'll plead for you,
As for my patron, stand you so assur'd,   155
As firmly as yourself were still in place;
Yea, and perhaps with more successful words

131 **grace** a favor. 134 **seen** instructed. 143 **proper stripling** fine
young man (ironical). 144 **note** memorandum. 146 **at any hand**
in any case. 150 **paper** i.e. note; cf. l. 144. 151 **them** i.e. the books;
cf. l. 146. 156 **as yourself** as if you yourself. **in place** present.

Than you unless you were a scholar, sir.

Gremio. O! this learning, what a thing it is.

Grumio. O! this woodcock, what an ass it is.　160

Petruchio. Peace, sirrah!

Hortensio. Grumio, mum! God save you, Signior
　　Gremio!

Gremio. And you are well met, Signior Hortensio.

Trow you whither I am going? To Baptista Minola.

I promis'd to inquire carefully　165

About a schoolmaster for the fair Bianca,

And, by good fortune, I have lighted well

On this young man; for learning and behavior

Fit for her turn; well read in poetry

And other books, good ones, I warrant ye.　170

Hortensio. 'Tis well: and I have met a gentleman

Hath promis'd me to help me to another,

A fine musician to instruct our mistress:

So shall I no whit be behind in duty

To fair Bianca, so belov'd of me.　175

Gremio. Belov'd of me, and that my deeds shall
　　prove.

Grumio. And that his bags shall prove.

Hortensio. Gremio, 'tis now no time to vent our
　　love.

Listen to me, and if you speak me fair

I'll tell you news indifferent good for either.　180

Here is a gentleman whom by chance I met,

Upon agreement from us to his liking,

Will undertake to woo curst Katherine;

Yea, and to marry her if her dowry please.

160 **woodcock** bird easily caught, hence symbol of stupidity. 164
trow know. 172 **help me** F *help one.* 177 **bags** moneybags. 178
vent express. 180 **indifferent** equally. 181 **gentleman** disyllabic
here, 'gemman.' 182 **upon agreement** on terms.

Gremio. So said, so done, is well. 185
Hortensio, have you told him all her faults?

Petruchio. I know she is an irksome, brawling scold:
If that be all, masters, I hear no harm.

Gremio. No, sayst me so, friend? What countryman?

Petruchio. Born in Verona, old Antonio's son: 190
My father dead, my fortune lives for me;
And I do hope good days and long to see.

Gremio. O, sir, such a life, with such a wife, were
strange!
But if you have a stomach, to't a God's name:
You shall have me assisting you in all. 195
But will you woo this wildcat?

Petruchio.   Will I live?

Grumio. [*Aside.*] Will he woo her? ay, or I'll hang
her.

Petruchio. Why came I hither but to that intent?
Think you a little din can daunt mine ears?
Have I not in my time heard lions roar? 200
Have I not heard the sea, puff'd up with winds,
Rage like an angry boar chafed with sweat?
Have I not heard great ordnance in the field
And heaven's artillery thunder in the skies?
Have I not in a pitched battle heard 205
Loud larums, neighing steeds, and trumpets' clang?
And do you tell me of a woman's tongue,
That gives not half so great a blow to hear
As will a chestnut in a farmer's fire? 209
Tush, tush! fear boys with bugs.

191 **Antonio's** F *Butonio's*. 194 **a** in. 202 **chafed** heated, irritated.
203 **ordnance** cannon. 204 **heaven's** monosyllable, **artillery** tri-
syllable. 206 **larums** alarms. 210 **fear** frighten. **bugs** bogeymen.
30

Grumio. [*Aside.*]   For he fears none.
Gremio. Hortensio, hark:
This gentleman is happily arriv'd,
My mind presumes, for his own good and ours.
   Hortensio. I promis'd we would be contributors,
And bear his charge of wooing, whatsoere.   215
   Gremio. And so we will, provided that he win her.
   Grumio. [*Aside.*] I would I were as sure of a good
      dinner.

Enter Tranio brave, and Biondello.

Tranio. Gentlemen, God save you! If I may be bold,
Tell me, I beseech you, which is the readiest way
To the house of Signior Baptista Minola?   220
   Biondello. He that has the two fair daughters: is't
      he you mean?
   Tranio. Even he, Biondello!
   Gremio. Hark you, sir; you mean not her to—
   Tranio. Perhaps, him and her, sir: what have you
      to do?
   Petruchio. Not her that chides, sir, at any hand, I
      pray.   225
   Tranio. I love no chiders, sir. Biondello, let's away.
   Lucentio. Well begun, Tranio.
   Hortensio.   Sir, a word ere you
      go:
Are you a suitor to the maid you talk of, yea or no?
   Tranio. And if I be, sir, is it any offence?
   Gremio. No, if without more words you will get you
      hence.   230
   Tranio. Why, sir, I pray, are not the streets as free
For me as for you?

213 ours F *yours.* 215 **charge** expense. SD **brave** finely dressed.

Gremio.　　　　　But so is not she.

Tranio. For what reason, I beseech you?

Gremio. For this reason, if you'll know,
That she's the choice love of Signior Gremio.　　235

Hortensio. That she's the chosen of Signior Hortensio.

Tranio. Softly, my masters! if you be gentlemen
Do me this right; hear me with patience.
Baptista is a noble gentleman
To whom my father is not all unknown,　　240
And were his daughter fairer than she is
She may more suitors have, and me for one.
Fair Leda's daughter had a thousand wooers;
Then well one more may fair Bianca have,
And so she shall; Lucentio shall make one　　245
Though Paris came in hope to speed alone.

Gremio. What! this gentleman will out-talk us all.

Lucentio. Sir, give him head. I know he'll prove a
  jade.

Petruchio. Hortensio, to what end are all these
  words?

Hortensio. Sir, let me be so bold as ask you,　　250
Did you yet ever see Baptista's daughter?

Tranio. No, sir; but hear I do that he hath two,
The one as famous for a scolding tongue
As is the other for beauteous modesty.　　254

Petruchio. Sir, sir, the first's for me; let her go by.

Gremio. Yea, leave that labor to great Hercules
And let it be more than Alcides' twelve.

Petruchio. Sir, understand you this of me in sooth:

243 **Leda's daughter** Helen of Troy. 244 **one more** i.e. than she
now has. 246 **Paris** Trojan prince who won Helen from her husband, King Menelaus. **came** were to come. **speed** succeed. 248
jade worthless nag. 257 **Alcides'** Hercules N.

The youngest daughter, whom you hearken for,
Her father keeps from all access of suitors   260
And will not promise her to any man
Until the elder sister first be wed;
The younger then is free, and not before.

  Tranio. If it be so, sir, that you are the man
Must stead us all, and me amongst the rest;   265
And if you break the ice and do this feat,
Achieve the elder, set the younger free
For our access, whose hap shall be to have her
Will not so graceless be to be ingrate.

  Hortensio. Sir, you say well, and well you do con-
      ceive;   270
And since you do profess to be a suitor
You must, as we do, gratify this gentleman
To whom we all rest generally beholding.

  Tranio. Sir, I shall not be slack: in sign whereof,
Please ye we may contrive this afternoon   275
And quaff carouses to our mistress' health
And do as adversaries do in law,
Strive mightily but eat and drink as friends.

  Grumio.
  Biondello. } O excellent motion! Fellows, let's be
         gone.

  Hortensio. The motion's good indeed, and be it
    so:—   280
Petruchio, I shall be your *ben venuto.*   *Exeunt.*

---

259 **hearken** lie in wait, long. 265 **stead** help. 266 **feat** F *seeke.*
268 **whose hap shall be** whoever has the good luck. 269 **to as**
to. **ingrate** ungrateful. 272 **gratify** reward. 273 **generally** read
'gen'rally.' 275 **contrive** while away. 276 **carouses** full glasses
of liquor. 281 **I . . . venuto** I shall sponsor you, see to your
reception.

[*Act II*

SCENE 1]

Enter Katherina and Bianca [with her hands tied].

Bianca. Good sister, wrong me not nor wrong your-
    self
To make a bondmaid and a slave of me;
That I disdain: but for these other gawds,
Unbind my hands, I'll pull them off myself,
Yea, all my raiment, to my petticoat;   5
Or what you will command me will I do,
So well I know my duty to my elders.
  Katherina. Of all thy suitors, here I charge thee,
    tell
Whom thou lov'st best: see thou dissemble not.
  Bianca. Believe me, sister, of all the men alive   10
I never yet beheld that special face
Which I could fancy more than any other.
  Katherina. Minion, thou liest. Is't not Hortensio?
  Bianca. If you affect him, sister, here I swear
I'll plead for you myself but you shall have him.   15
  Katherina. O! then, belike, you fancy riches more:
You will have Gremio to keep you fair.
  Bianca. Is it for him you do envy me so?
Nay, then you jest and now I well perceive
You have but jested with me all this while.   20
I prithee, sister Kate, untie my hands.

3 **gawds** adornments; F *goods*. 13 **Minion** minx. 17 **fair** richly
dressed. 18 **envy** (stressed — $\smile$) dislike.
    34

Katherina. If that be jest then all the rest was so.
Strikes her.

Enter Baptista.

Baptista. Why, how now, dame! whence grows this
insolence?
Bianca, stand aside. Poor girl! she weeps.
Go ply thy needle; meddle not with her.   25
For shame, thou hilding of a divelish spirit,
Why dost thou wrong her that did nere wrong thee?
When did she cross thee with a bitter word?
Katherina. Her silence flouts me and I'll be reveng'd.
Flies after Bianca.
Baptista. What! in my sight? Bianca, get thee in.
Exit [Bianca].
Katherina. What! will you not suffer me? Nay, now
I see   31
She is your treasure, she must have a husband;
I must dance barefoot on her wedding day,
And, for your love to her, lead apes in hell.
Talk not to me: I will go sit and weep   35
Till I can find occasion of revenge.   [*Exit.*]
Baptista. Was ever gentleman thus griev'd as I?
But who comes here?

*Enter Gremio, [with] Lucentio in the habit of a
mean man; Petruchio, with [Hortensio as a Musician; and] Tranio, with his boy [Biondello]
bearing a lute and books.*

Gremio. Good morrow, neighbor Baptista.

26 **hilding** wretch. 33 **dance barefoot on her wedding day** N. 34
lead apes in hell proverbial destiny of old maids. Cf. *Much Ado
About Nothing* II.1.40.

Baptista. Good morrow, neighbor Gremio. God save you, gentlemen!   41

Petruchio. And you, good sir. Pray, have you not a
    daughter
Call'd Katherina, fair and virtuous?

Baptista. I have a daughter, sir, call'd Katherina.

Gremio. You are too blunt: go to it orderly.   45

Petruchio. You wrong me, Signior Gremio: give me
    leave.
I am a gentleman of Verona, sir,
That, hearing of her beauty and her wit,
Her affability and bashful modesty,
Her wondrous qualities and mild behavior,   50
Am bold to show myself a forward guest
Within your house, to make mine eye the witness
Of that report which I so oft have heard.
And, for an entrance to my entertainment,
I do present you with a man of mine,   55
                [Presenting Hortensio.]
Cunning in music and the mathematics,
To instruct her fully in those sciences,
Whereof I know she is not ignorant.
Accept of him, or else you do me wrong:
His name is Licio, born in Mantua.   60

Baptista. Y'are welcome, sir; and he, for your good
    sake.
But for my daughter Katherina, this I know,
She is not for your turn, the more my grief.

Petruchio. I see you do not mean to part with her
Or else you like not of my company.   65

Baptista. Mistake me not; I speak but as I find.
Whence are you, sir? what may I call your name?

57 **To instruct** read 't'instruct.' 63 **turn** purpose. 65 **like not of**
do not care for.

36

Petruchio. Petruchio is my name, Antonio's son,
A man well known throughout all Italy.

Baptista. I know him well: you are welcome for his
    sake.   70

Gremio. Saving your tale, Petruchio, I pray,
Let us, that are poor petitioners, speak too.
Bacare! you are marvelous forward.

Petruchio. O, pardon me, Signior Gremio, I would
    fain be doing.

Gremio. I doubt it not, sir; but you will curse your
    wooing.   75
Neighbor, this is a gift very grateful, I am sure of
it. To express the like kindness myself, that have
been more kindly beholding to you than any, freely
give unto you this young scholar, [*Presenting Lucentio.*] that hath been long studying at Rheims; as
cunning in Greek, Latin, and other languages, as the
other in music and mathematics. His name is Cambio; pray accept his service.   83

Baptista. A thousand thanks, Signior Gremio; Welcome, good Cambio.—[*To Tranio.*] But, gentle sir,
methinks you walk like a stranger: may I be so bold
to know the cause of your coming?

Tranio. Pardon me, sir, the boldness is mine own,
That, being a stranger in this city here,
Do make myself a suitor to your daughter,   90
Unto Bianca, fair and virtuous.
Nor is your firm resolve unknown to me
In the preferment of the eldest sister.
This liberty is all that I request,

71–3 saving . . . forward F sets as prose. 71 **Saving** with all due
respect. 73 **Bacare** back (burlesque Latin). **marvelous** marvel-
ously. 75–6 your wooing. **Neighbor** F *your wooing neighbors*. 76–87
Neighbor . . . your coming F sets as verse. 79 **you** F omits.

That, upon knowledge of my parentage, 95
I may have welcome 'mongst the rest that woo
And free access and favor as the rest.
And, toward the education of your daughters
I here bestow a simple instrument,
And this small packet of Greek and Latin books: 100
If you accept them, then their worth is great.
  Baptista. Lucentio is your name, of whence, I pray?
  Tranio. Of Pisa, sir; son to Vincentio.
  Baptista. A mighty man of Pisa; by report
I know him well. You are very welcome, sir. 105
[*To Hortensio.*] Take you that lute, [*To Lucentio.*]
    and you the set of books;
You shall go see your pupils presently.
Holla, within!

Enter a Servant.

              Sirrah, lead these gentlemen
To my daughters and tell them both
These are their tutors: bid them use them well. 110
              [*Exit Servant, with Lucentio and
              Hortensio, Biondello following.*]
We will go walk a little in the orchard
And then to dinner. You are passing welcome
And so I pray you all to think yourselves.
  Petruchio. Signior Baptista, my business asketh
    haste
And every day I cannot come to woo. 115
You knew my father well, and in him me,
Left solely heir to all his lands and goods,
Which I have better'd rather than decreas'd:
Then tell me, if I get your daughter's love

111 **orchard** garden. 112 **passing** exceedingly.

What dowry shall I have with her to wife?   120

Baptista. After my death the one half of my lands,
And in possession twenty thousand crowns.

Petruchio. And, for that dowry, I'll assure her of
Her widowhood, be it that she survive me,
In all my lands and leases whatsoever.   125
Let specialties be therefore drawn between us
That covenants may be kept on either hand.

Baptista. Ay, when the special thing is well obtain'd,
That is, her love; for that is all in all.

Petruchio. Why, that is nothing; for I tell you, father,   130
I am as peremptory as she proud-minded;
And where two raging fires meet together
They do consume the thing that feeds their fury:
Though little fire grows great with little wind,
Yet extreme gusts will blow out fire and all;   135
So I to her, and so she yields to me;
For I am rough and woo not like a babe.

Baptista. Well mayst thou woo and happy be thy speed!
But be thou arm'd for some unhappy words.

Petruchio. Ay, to the proof; as mountains are for winds,   140
That shake not, though they blow perpetually.

Enter Hortensio, with his head broke.

Baptista. How now, my friend! why dost thou look so pale?

124 **widowhood** widow's share of estate. 126 **specialties** specific contracts. 131 **peremptory** stressed $\acute{-} — \grave{-} —$. 135 **extreme** stressed $\acute{-} —$. 138 **speed** fortune. 140 **to the proof** as if in proved (i.e. tested) armor. 141 **shake** F *shakes.*

Hortensio. For fear, I promise you, if I look pale.

Baptista. What, will my daughter prove a good
    musician?

Hortensio. I think she'll sooner prove a soldier. 145
Iron may hold with her but never lutes.

Baptista. Why, then thou canst not break her to
    the lute?

Hortensio. Why, no; for she hath broke the lute
    to me.
I did but tell her she mistook her frets
And bow'd her hand to teach her fingering; 150
When, with a most impatient divelish spirit,
'Frets, call you these?' quoth she; 'I'll fume with
    them';
And, with that word, she stroke me on the head,
And through the instrument my pate made way.
And there I stood amazed for a while 155
As on a pillory, looking through the lute,
While she did call me rascal, fiddler,
And twangling Jack, with twenty such vilde terms
As had she studied to misuse me so. 159

Petruchio. Now, by the world, it is a lusty wench!
I love her ten times more than ere I did:
O! how I long to have some chat with her!

Baptista. [*To Hortensio.*] Well, go with me, and be
    not so discomfited.
Proceed in practice with my younger daughter;
She's apt to learn and thankful for good turns. 165
Signior Petruchio, will you go with us

145 **soldier** three syllables here. 146 **hold with** resist. 149 **frets**
ridges on the neck of the lute where the strings are pressed.
150 **bow'd** bent. 152 **Frets . . . fume with them** plays on 'fret'
and 'fume.' 153 **stroke** struck. 158 **twangling** twanging. **vilde** vile.
159 **As had . . .** i.e. as if she had made special preparation to
abuse me. 160 **lusty** lively. 165 **apt** ready.

Or shall I send my daughter Kate to you?
> *Exit [Baptista, with Gremio, Tranio, and
> Hortensio]. Manet Petruchio.*

Petruchio. I pray you do; I will attend her here
And woo her with some spirit when she comes.
Say that she rail; why then I'll tell her plain   170
She sings as sweetly as a nightingale:
Say that she frown; I'll say she looks as clear
As morning roses newly wash'd with dew:
Say she be mute and will not speak a word;
Then I'll commend her volubility,   175
And say she uttereth piercing eloquence.
If she do bid me pack I'll give her thanks
As though she bid me stay by her a week;
If she deny to wed I'll crave the day   179
When I shall ask the banes, and when be married.
But here she comes; and now, Petruchio, speak.

Enter Katherina.

Good morrow, Kate; for that's your name, I hear.
Katherina. Well have you heard, but something
    hard of hearing:
They call me Katerina that do talk of me.
Petruchio. You lie, in faith; for you are call'd plain
    Kate,   185
And bonny Kate, and sometimes Kate the curst;
But, Kate, the prettiest Kate in Christendom;
Kate of Kate-Hall, my super-dainty Kate,
For dainties are all Kates: and therefore, Kate,
Take this of me, Kate of my consolation;   190
Hearing thy mildness prais'd in every town,
Thy virtues spoke of, and thy beauty sounded—

---

176 **uttereth** read 'utt'reth.' 177 **pack** be off. 179 **deny** refuse.
180 **banes** banns. 183–192 **hard . . . sounded** N. 188 **Kate-Hall** N.

Yet not so deeply as to thee belongs—
Myself am mov'd to woo thee for my wife.

   Katherina. Mov'd! in good time: let him that mov'd
    you hether   195
Remove you hence. I knew you at the first,
You were a movable.

   Petruchio.   Why, what's a movable?

   Katherina. A joint stool.

   Petruchio.   Thou hast hit it: come sit
    on me.   198

   Katherina. Asses are made to bear and so are you.

   Petruchio. Women are made to bear and so are you.

   Katherina. No such jade as you, if me you mean.

   Petruchio. Alas! good Kate, I will not burthen thee;
For, knowing thee to be but young and light—

   Katherina. Too light for such a swain as you to
    catch
And yet as heavy as my weight should be.   205

   Petruchio. Should be! should—buzz!

   Katherina.   Well tane, and
    like a buzzard.

   Petruchio. O slow-wing'd turtle! shall a buzzard
    take thee?

   Katherina. Ay, for a turtle, as he takes a buzzard.

   Petruchio. Come, come, you wasp; i' faith you are
    too angry.   209

   Katherina. If I be waspish best beware my sting.

   Petruchio. My remedy is then to pluck it out.

---

195 **in good time** indeed 197 **movable** pun on 'piece of furniture.'
198 **joint stool** stool made by a joiner. 199–200 **bear** i.e. 1) a man,
2) children. 201 **jade** worthless nag, worthless person. 204 **swain**
young rustic. 206 **be** pun on 'bee.' **buzz** 1) hum, 2) tush. **buzzard**
1) kind of hawk, 2) blockhead, 3) large insect. 207 **turtle** turtle-
dove. 208 **Ay, for a turtle** . . . N.

Katherina. Ay, if the fool could find it where it lies.

Petruchio. Who knows not where a wasp does wear
   his sting?

In his tail.

Katherina. In his tongue.

Petruchio.   Whose tongue?

Katherina. Yours, if you talk of tales; and so farewell.   215

Petruchio. What! with my tongue in your tail? nay,
   come again.

Good Kate, I am a gentleman.

Katherina.   That I'll try.

                   She strikes him.

Petruchio. I swear I'll cuff you if you strike again.

Katherina. So may you lose your arms:

If you strike me you are no gentleman,   220
And if no gentleman, why then no arms.

Petruchio. A herald, Kate? O! put me in thy books.

Katherina. What is your crest? a coxcomb?

Petruchio. A combless cock, so Kate will be my hen.

Katherina. No cock of mine; you crow too like a
   craven.   225

Petruchio. Nay, come, Kate, come; you must not
   look so sour.

Katherina. It is my fashion when I see a crab.

Petruchio. Why, here's no crab, and therefore look
   not sour.

Katherina. There is, there is.   229

Petruchio. Then show it me.

---

215 **talk of tales** talk idly. 219 **arms** pun on 'coat of arms.' 222
herald and hence authority on heraldry. **books** heraldic registers,
with pun on 'in your good books.' 223 **coxcomb** badge of the court
fool. 224 **combless** gentle, with crest cut down. 225 **craven**
cowardly (cock-fighting term). 227 **crab** crab apple.

Katherina. Had I a glass I would.

Petruchio. What, you mean my face?

Katherina. Well aim'd of such a young one.

Petruchio. Now, by Saint George, I am too young for you.

Katherina. Yet you are wither'd.

Petruchio. 'Tis with cares.

Katherina. I care not.

Petruchio. Nay, hear you, Kate: in sooth you scape not so.

Katherina. I chafe you if I tarry: let me go.   235

Petruchio. No, not a whit: I find you passing gentle.
'Twas told me you were rough and coy and sullen,
And now I find report a very liar;
For thou art pleasant, gamesome, passing courteous,
But slow in speech, yet sweet as springtime flowers.
Thou canst not frown, thou canst not look a sconce,
Nor bite the lip as angry wenches will,
Nor hast thou pleasure to be cross in talk;
But thou with mildness entertain'st thy wooers,
With gentle conference, soft and affable.   245
Why does the world report that Kate doth limp?
O sland'rous world! Kate, like the hazel-twig
Is straight and slender, and as brown in hue
As hazelnuts and sweeter than the kernels.
O! let me see thee walk: thou dost not halt.   250

Katherina. Go, fool, and whom thou keep'st command.

231 **aim'd of** guessed for. 234 **scape** escape. 235 **chafe** irritate.
237 **coy** haughty. 241 **a sconce** askance. 245 **conference** conversation. 250 **halt** limp. 251 **whom thou keep'st command** i.e. tell
your servants (not me) what to do.

Petruchio. Did ever Dian so become a grove
As Kate this chamber with her princely gait?
O! be thou Dian and let her be Kate,
And then let Kate be chaste and Dian sportful! 255
  Katherina. Where did you study all this goodly
    speech?
  Petruchio. It is extempore, from my mother-wit.
  Katherina. A witty mother! witless else her son.
  Petruchio. Am I not wise?
  Katherina.   Yes; keep you warm.
  Petruchio. Marry, so I mean, sweet Katherine, in
    thy bed; 260
And therefore, setting all this chat aside,
Thus in plain terms: your father hath consented
That you shall be my wife, your dowry 'greed on;
And will you, nill you, I will marry you.
Now, Kate, I am a husband for your turn; 265
For, by this light, whereby I see thy beauty—
Thy beauty that doth make me like thee well—
Thou must be married to no man but me.

    Enter Baptista, Gremio, [and] Tranio.

For I am he am born to tame you, Kate,
And bring you from a wild Kate to a Kate 270
Conformable as other household Kates.
Here comes your father: never make denial;
I must and will have Katherine to my wife.
  Baptista. Now, Signior Petruchio, how speed you
    with my daughter?
  Petruchio. How but well, sir? how but well? 275

252 **Dian** Diana, chaste goddess of the hunt. 259 **warm** with
reference to the proverbial expression 'wit enough to keep oneself
warm'; as we should say 'enough sense to come in out of the rain.'
264 **nill you** will you not. 270 **wild Kate** pun on 'cat' as in l. 271.

It were impossible I should speed amiss.

Baptista. Why, how now, daughter Katherine! in
    your dumps.

Katherina. Call you me daughter? now, I promise
    you

You have show'd a tender fatherly regard

To wish me wed to one half lunatic,   280

A madcap ruffian and a swearing Jack

That thinks with oaths to face the matter out.

Petruchio. Father, 'tis thus: yourself and all the
    world

That talk'd of her have talk'd amiss of her.

If she be curst it is for policy,   285

For she's not froward but modest as the dove,

She is not hot but temperate as the morn;

For patience she will prove a second Grissel

And Roman Lucrece for her chastity;   289

And to conclude, we have 'greed so well together

That upon Sunday is the wedding day.

Katherina. I'll see thee hang'd on Sunday first.

Gremio. Hark, Petruchio: she says she'll see thee
    hang'd first.

Tranio. Is this your speeding? nay, then good night
    our part!

Petruchio. Be patient, gentlemen, I choose her for
    myself;   295

If she and I be pleas'd, what's that to you?

'Tis bargain'd 'twixt us twain, being alone,

That she shall still be curst in company.

I tell you, 'tis incredible to believe

277 **in your dumps** downcast. 278 **promise** assure. 279 **You have**
read 'you've.' 282 **face** brazen. 285 **for policy** with calculated
purpose. 286 **froward** perverse. 287 **temperate** read 'temp'rate.'
288–289 **Grissel . . . Lucrece** N. 290 **we have** read 'we've.' 294
speeding success.

How much she loves me. O! the kindest Kate,   300
She hung about my neck, and kiss on kiss
She vied so fast, protesting oath on oath,
That in a twink she won me to her love.
O! you are novices; 'tis a world to see
How tame, when men and women are alone,   305
A meacock wretch can make the curstest shrew.
Give me thy hand, Kate: I will unto Venice
To buy apparel 'gainst the wedding day.
Provide the feast, father, and bid the guests;
I will be sure my Katherine shall be fine.   310
    Baptista. I know not what to say; but give me your
        hands.
God send you joy, Petruchio! 'tis a match.
    Gremio. }
    Tranio. } Amen, say we: we will be witnesses.
    Petruchio. Father, and wife, and gentlemen, adieu.
I will to Venice; Sunday comes apace.   315
We will have rings and things and fine array;
And, kiss me, Kate, we will be married a' Sunday.
                    Exeunt Petruchio and Katherine.
    Gremio. Was ever match clapp'd up so suddenly?
    Baptista. Faith, gentlemen, now I play a mar-
        chant's part
And venture madly on a desperate mart.   320
    Tranio. 'Twas a commodity lay fretting by you;
'Twill bring you gain or perish on the seas.
    Baptista. The gain I seek is quiet in the match.

---

302 **vied so fast** i.e. rivaled me in eagerness to exchange kisses.
303 **twink** twinkling. 304 **world** worth a world; i.e. wonderful.
306 **meacock** meet or cowardly. 310 **fine** handsomely dressed.
311 **give me your hands** i.e. to join them in betrothal. 318 **clapp'd
up** arranged. 319 **marchant's** merchant's. 320 **mart** market. 321
fretting of cloth ravaged by moths, hence 'wasting away,' with
pun on Kate's fretful temper.

Gremio. No doubt but he hath got a quiet catch.
But now, Baptista, to your younger daughter: 325
Now is the day we long have looked for;
I am your neighbor, and was suitor first.
  Tranio. And I am one that love Bianca more
Than words can witness or your thoughts can guess.
  Gremio. Youngling, thou canst not love so dear as I.
  Tranio. Greybeard, thy love doth freeze.
  Gremio.   But thine
        doth fry. 331
Skipper, stand back, 'tis age that nourisheth.
  Tranio. But youth in ladies' eyes that flourisheth.
  Baptista. Content you, gentlemen; I will compound
        this strife:
'Tis deeds must win the prize, and he, of both, 335
That can assure my daughter greatest dower
Shall have my Bianca's love.
Say, Signior Gremio, what can you assure her?
  Gremio. First, as you know, my house within the
        city
Is richly furnished with plate and gold: 340
Basins and ewers to lave her dainty hands;
My hangings all of Tyrian tapestry;
In ivory coffers I have stuff'd my crowns;
In cypress chests my arras counterpoints,
Costly apparel, tents, and canopies. 345
Fine linen, Turkey cushions boss'd with pearl,

332 **Skipper** one whose gait reveals lack of maturity and dignity, 'prancer.' 334 **Content you** be calm. **compound** settle. 335 **he, of both** whichever of the two. 342 **Tyrian** purple, dark red. 344 **arras counterpoints** tapestry woven in squares of contrasting colors, made in Arras, France. 345 **tents and canopies** bed-hangings. 346 **Turkey cushions boss'd with pearl** oriental cushions embroidered with pearls.

Valance of Venice gold in needlework,
Pewter and brass, and all things that belong
To house or housekeeping. Then, at my farm
I have a hundred milch-kine to the pail,   350
Six score fat oxen standing in my stalls
And all things answerable to this portion.
Myself am strook in years, I must confess;
And if I die tomorrow, this is hers,
If whilst I live she will be only mine.   355
   Tranio. That 'only' came well in. Sir, list to me:
I am my father's heir and only son,
If I may have your daughter to my wife
I'll leave her houses three or four as good,
Within rich Pisa walls, as any one   360
Old Signior Gremio has in Padua;
Besides two thousand ducats by the year
Of fruitful land, all which shall be her jointer.
What, have I pinch'd you, Signior Gremio?   364
   Gremio. Two thousand ducats by the year of land!
My land amounts not to so much in all:
That she shall have besides an argosy
That now is lying in Marcellus' road.
What, have I chok'd you with an argosy?   369
   Tranio. Gremio, 'tis known my father hath no less
Than three great argosies, besides two galliasses
And twelve tight galleys; these I will assure her
And twice as much, whatere thou offer'st next.

347 **Valance** fringes, draperies of bed or couch. 348 **belong** F
belongs. 350 **milch-kine to the pail** cows giving milk for the dairy
(not to calves). 352 **answerable to this portion** in agreement with
this marriage settlement. 353 **strook** struck, 'advanced.' 362 **ducats**
Venetian coins. 363 **jointer** jointure, marriage settlement. 367
That i.e. the whole value of my land. **argosy** large merchant-ship.
368 **Marcellus'** Marseilles'. **road** harbor. 371 **galliasses** large
galleys.

Gremio. Nay, I have off'red all, I have no more;
And she can have no more than all I have.   375
If you like me, she shall have me and mine.

Tranio. Why, then the maid is mine from all the
world
By your firm promise. Gremio is outvied.

Baptista. I must confess your offer is the best
And, let your father make her the assurance,   380
She is your own; else, you must pardon me,
If you should die before him, where's her dower?

Tranio. That's but a cavil: he is old, I young.

Gremio. And may not young men die as well as old?

Baptista. Well, gentlemen,   385
I am thus resolv'd. On Sunday next, you know,
My daughter Katherine is to be married:
Now, on the Sunday following, shall Bianca
Be bride to you if you make this assurance;
If not, to Signior Gremio: 390
And so I take my leave and thank you both.   *Exit.*

Gremio. Adieu, good neighbor. Now I fear thee not:
Sirrah young gamester, your father were a fool
To give thee all and in his waning age
Set foot under thy table. Tut! a toy!   395
An old Italian fox is not so kind, my boy.   *Exit.*

Tranio. A vengeance on your crafty wither'd hide!
Yet I have fac'd it with a card of ten.
'Tis in my head to do my master good:
I see no reason, but suppos'd Lucentio   400

378 **outvied** outbid. 380 **assurance** guarantee. 383 **cavil** trifling
argument. 386 **I am read** 'I'm.' 393 **gamester** adventurer. **were**
would be. 395 **Set foot under thy table** live as your pensioner.
a toy nonsense. 398 **fac'd . . . ten** bluff'd him; making him think
my ten spot was a face card, a term from the game of primero.

Must get a father, called 'suppos'd Vincentio';
And that's a wonder: fathers commonly
Do get their children, but in this case of wooing
A child shall get a sire if I fail not of my cunning.

Exit.

403 **get** beget.

Act III

[SCENE 1]

Enter Lucentio, Hortensio, and Bianca.

Lucentio. Fiddler, forbear; you grow too forward, sir.
Have you so soon forgot the entertainment
Her sister Katherine welcom'd you withal?

Hortensio. But, wrangling pedant, know this lady is
The patroness of heavenly harmony;   5
Then give me leave to have prerogative,
And when in music we have spent an hour
Your lecture shall have leisure for as much.

Lucentio. Preposterous ass, that never read so far
To know the cause why music was ordain'd!   10
Was it not to refresh the mind of man
After his studies or his usual pain?
Then give me leave to read philosophy,
And while I pause, serve in your harmony.

Hortensio. Sirrah, I will not bear these braves of thine.   15

Bianca. Why, gentlemen, you do me double wrong
To strive for that which resteth in my choice.
I am no breeching scholar in the schools;

Act III, Scene 1 F *Actus Tertia.* 4 know this lady is F *this is* N.
6 prerogative precedence. 12 pain toil. 15 braves pretensions. 18
breeching scholar schoolboy liable to whipping.

I'll not be tied to hours nor 'pointed times,
But learn my lessons as I please myself. 20
And, to cut off all strife, here sit we down;
Take you your instrument, play you the whiles;
His lecture will be done ere you have tun'd.

Hortensio. You'll leave his lecture when I am in
tune? 24

Lucentio. That will be never; tune your instrument.

Bianca. Where left we last?

Lucentio. Here, madam: —

'Hic ibat Simois; hic est Sigeria tellus;
Hic steterat Priami regia celsa senis.'

Bianca. Conster them. 30

Lucentio. Hic ibat, as I told you before, *Simois,* I
am Lucentio, *hic est,* son unto Vincentio of Pisa,
Sigeria tellus, disguised thus to get your love; *Hic
steterat,* and that Lucentio that comes a wooing,
Priami, is my man Tranio, *regia,* bearing my port,
celsa senis, that we might beguile the old pantaloon.

Hortensio. Madam, my instrument's in tune. 37

Bianca. Let's hear. — O fie! the treble jars.

Lucentio. Spit in the hole, man, and tune again.

Bianca. Now let me see if I can conster it: *Hic ibat
Simois,* I know you not, *hic est Sigeria tellus,* I trust
you not; *Hic steterat Priami,* take heed he hear us
not, *regia,* presume not, *celsa senis,* despair not.

Hortensio. Madam, 'tis now in tune.

Lucentio.   All but the
bass.

Hortensio. The bass is right; 'tis the base knave
that jars. 45

19 'pointed appointed. 22 the whiles meanwhile. 28–9 Hic ibat
. . . celsa senis N. 30 conster construe. 35 port appearance 36
pantaloon cf. N. to I, 3, 47 SD. 37–39 N.

[*Aside.*] How fiery and forward our pedant is!
Now, for my life, the knave doth court my love;
Pedascule, I'll watch you better yet.

  Bianca. In time I may believe, yet I mistrust.

  Lucentio. Mistrust it not; for, sure, Æacides   50
Was Ajax, call'd so from his grandfather.

  Bianca. I must believe my master; else, I promise
    you,
I should be arguing still upon that doubt;
But let it rest. Now, Licio, to you.
Good master, take it not unkindly, pray,   55
That I have been thus pleasant with you both.

  Hortensio. You may go walk and give me leave a
    while;
My lessons make no music in three parts.

  Lucentio. Are you so formal, sir? [*Aside.*] Well, I
    must wait
And watch withal; for, but I be deceiv'd,   60
Our fine musician groweth amorous.

  Hortensio. Madam, before you touch the instrument
To learn the order of my fingering,
I must begin with rudiments of art
To teach you gamouth in a briefer sort,   65
More pleasant, pithy, and effectual,
Than hath been taught by any of my trade;
And there it is in writing, fairly drawn.

  Bianca. Why, I am past my gamouth long ago.

  Hortensio. Yet read the gamouth of Hortensio.   70

  Bianca.

>   ' "Gamouth" I am, the ground of all accord,
>   "A re," to plead Hortensio's passion;

46–49 N. 48 **Pedascule** pedant (synthetic Latin). 50–51 N.
52–56 N. 60 **but** unless. 65 **gamouth** gamut, i.e. the diatonic
scale N. 71 **ground** beginning, basis.

"B mi," Bianca, take him for thy lord,
"C fa ut," that loves with all affection;
"D sol re," one cliffe, two notes have I; 75
"E la mi," show pity or I die.'

Call *you* this gamouth? tut, I like it not.
Old fashions please me best; I am not so nice
To change true rules for odd inventions.

Enter a Messenger.

Messenger. Mistress, your father prays you leave
your books 80
And help to dress your sister's chamber up;
You know tomorrow is the wedding day.
Bianca. Farewell, sweet masters both; I must be
gone. [*Exeunt Bianca and Messenger.*]
Lucentio. Faith, mistress, then I have no cause to
stay. [*Exit.*]
Hortensio. But I have cause to pry into this pedant.
Methinks he looks as though he were in love. 86
Yet if thy thoughts, Bianca, be so humble
To cast thy wand'ring eyes on every stale,
Seize thee that list; if once I find thee ranging,
Hortensio will be quit with thee by changing. *Exit.*

73 **B mi** F *Beeme.* 75 **cliffe** clef (key in music). 78 **nice** capricious.
79 **to** as to. **change** F *charge.* **odd** F *old.* 80 **Messenger** F *Nicke* N.
88 **stale** lure, decoy. 89 **Seize thee that list** let them take thee that
will. **ranging** roving. 90 **be quit** get even. **by changing** by loving
another.

[SCENE 2]

Enter Baptista, Gremio, Tranio, Katherina, Bianca [Lucentio,] and others, attendants.

Baptista. [*To Tranio.*] Signior Lucentio, this is
    the 'pointed day
That Katherine and Petruchio should be married,
And yet we hear not of our son-in-law.
What will be said? what mockery will it be
To want the bridegroom when the priest attends   5
To speak the ceremonial rites of marriage!
What says Lucentio to this shame of ours?
  Katherina. No shame but mine; I must, forsooth, be
    forc'd
To give my hand oppos'd against my heart
Unto a mad-brain rudesby, full of spleen,   10
Who woo'd in haste and means to wed at leisure.
I told you, I, he was a frantic fool,
Hiding his bitter jests in blunt behavior;
And to be noted for a merry man,   14
He'll woo a thousand, point the day of marriage,
Make friends, invite, and proclaim the banes;
Yet never means to wed where he hath woo'd.
Now must the world point at poor Katherine
And say, 'Lo! there is mad Petruchio's wife,
If it would please him come and marry her.'   20
  Tranio. Patience, good Katherine, and Baptista too.
Upon my life, Petruchio means but well,
Whatever fortune stays him from his word.

---

4 **mockery** read 'mock'ry.' 10 **rudesby** bumpkin. **spleen** impulsive
temper. 14 **noted for** known as. 15 **point** appoint. 16 **banes** banns.

Though he be blunt, I know him passing wise;
Though he be merry, yet withal he's honest.   25
   Katherina. Would Katherine had never seen him
      though!
        Exit weeping [*followed by Bianca and others*].
   Baptista. Go, girl: I cannot blame thee now to
      weep,
For such an injury would vex a very saint,
Much more a shrew of thy impatient humor.   29

Enter Biondello.

   Biondello. Master, master! news! and such old news
as you never heard of!
   Baptista. Is it new and old too? how may that be?
   Biondello. Why, is it not news to hear of Petru-
chio's coming?
   Baptista. Is he come?   35
   Biondello. Why, no, sir.
   Baptista. What then?
   Biondello. He is coming.
   Baptista. When will he be here?   39
   Biondello. When he stands where I am and sees you
there.
   Tranio. But, say, what to thine old news?   42
   Biondello. Why, Petruchio is coming, in a new hat
and an old jerkin; a pair of old breeches thrice
turn'd; a pair of boots that have been candle-cases,
one buckled, another lac'd; an old rusty sword tane
out of the town-armory, with a broken hilt, and
chapeless; with two broken points: his horse hipp'd

30 **old** rare; F omits N. 45 **candle-cases** i.e. worn out and used as
receptacles for candle ends. 48 **chapeless** the chape is the metal
tip at the end of the sheath. **points** garters. **hipp'd** lamed in
the hip.

with an old mothy saddle and stirrups of no kindred;
besides, possessed with the glanders and like to mose
in the chine; troubled with the lampass, infected with
the fashions, full of windgalls, sped with spavins,
rayed with the yellows, past cure of the fives, stark
spoil'd with the staggers, begnawn with the bots,
swayed in the back, and shoulder-shotten; near-
legg'd before, and with a half-chekt bit, and a head-
stall of sheep's leather, which, being restrain'd to
keep him from stumbling, hath been often burst and
now repaired with knots; one girth six times piec'd,
and a woman's crupper of velure, which hath two
letters for her name fairly set down in studs, and
here and there piec'd with packthread.   62

Baptista. Who comes with him?

Biondello. O, sir! his lackey, for all the world caparison'd like the horse; with a linen stock on one

49 **of no kindred** not matching. 50 **glanders** swellings under the
jaw. 50–51 **mose in the chine** a dark discharge from the nostrils (a
horse disease). 51 **lampass** infected mouth (in horses). 52 **fashions**
farcins, i.e. small tumors on horse's body. **windgalls** swelling on
fetlock joints. **spavins** a disease of the hock. 53 **rayed** befouled.
yellows kind of jaundice. **fives** (a)vives, i.e. swellings at base of
the ear. 53–54 **stark spoil'd with the staggers** a prey to a kind of
horse palsy. 54 **begnawn with the bots** gnawed by small intestinal
worms. 55 **swayed** with rolling gate, due to back strain; F *Waid*.
shoulder-shotten with dislocated shoulder. 55–56 **near-legg'd before** with forefeet that knock together. 56 **half-chekt** 'half-checked'
or 'half-cheeked,' loose. 56–57 **head-stall** part of the bridle sur-
rounding the head. **sheep's leather** inferior leather, not pigskin
as would become a person of consequence. **restrain'd** drawn
tight. 59 **piec'd** patched. 60 **crupper** strap fastened to back of
saddle and passing around the horse's tail. **velure** velvet. 64–65
caparison'd decked out. 65 **stock** stocking.

leg and a kersey boot-hose on the other, gart'red
with a red and blue list; an old hat, and the 'humor
of forty fancies' prick'd in't for a feather: a monster, a very monster in apparel, and not like a Chris-
tian footboy or a gentleman's lackey.   70

Tranio. 'Tis some odd humor pricks him to this
    fashion,
Yet oftentimes he goes but mean-apparell'd.

Baptista. I am glad he's come, howsoere he comes.

Biondello. Why, sir, he comes not.

Baptista. Didst thou not say he comes?   75

Biondello. Who? that Petruchio came?

Baptista. Ay, that Petruchio came.

Biondello. No, sir; I say his horse comes, with him
on his back.

Baptista. Why, that's all one.   80

Biondello.

> Nay, by Saint Jamy,
> I hold you a penny,
> A horse and a man
> Is more than one
> And yet not many.   85

Enter Petruchio and Grumio.

Petruchio. Come, where be these gallants? who is at
    home?

Baptista. You are welcome, sir.

Petruchio.   And yet I come not
    well.

66 **kersey boot-hose** coarse woollen stocking worn under the
riding boot. 67 **list** strip of cloth. 67–8 '**humor of forty fancies**'
parcel of ribbons tied together (instead of the conventional
feather) N. 70 **footboy** attendant in livery. 71 **pricks** drives. 82
hold bet. 86 **gallants** fine fellows.

Baptista. And yet you halt not.

Tranio.   Not so well appar-
    ell'd

As I wish you were.   89

Petruchio. Were it better, I should rush in thus.

But where is Kate? where is my lovely bride?

How does my father? Gentles, methinks you frown.

And wherefore gaze this goodly company

As if they saw some wondrous monument,

Some comet, or unusual prodigy?   95

Baptista. Why, sir, you know this is your wedding
    day.

First were we sad, fearing you would not come;

Now sadder that you come so unprovided.

Fie! doff this habit, shame to your estate,

An eyesore to our solemn festival.   100

Tranio. And tell us what occasion of import

Hath all so long detain'd you from your wife

And sent you hither so unlike yourself?

Petruchio. Tedious it were to tell and harsh to hear.

Sufficeth, I am come to keep my word   105

Though in some part enforced to digress;

Which, at more leisure, I will so excuse

As you shall well be satisfied with all.

But where is Kate? I stay too long from her;   109

The morning wears, 'tis time we were at church.

Tranio. See not your bride in these unrevent
    robes.

Go to my chamber; put on clothes of mine.

Petruchio. Not I, believe me; thus I'll visit her.

Baptista. But thus, I trust, you will not marry her.

88–9 **Not . . . were** set as one line in F. 92 **Gentles** gentlemen.
99 **habit** costume. **estate** social position. 106 **enforced to digress**
compelled to deviate from my promise (II.1.307–310).

60

Petruchio. Good sooth, even thus; therefore ha'
    done with words: 115
To me she's married, not unto my clothes.
Could I repair what she will wear in me
As I can change these poor accouterments,
'Twere well for Kate and better for myself.
But what a fool am I to chat with you   120
When I should bid good morrow to my bride
And seal the title with a lovely kiss!
                   Exit [with Grumio].
   Tranio. He hath some meaning in his mad attire.
We will persuade him, be it possible,
To put on better ere he go to church.   125
   Baptista. I'll after him and see the event of this.
           Exit [with Gremio and Attendants].
   Tranio. But to her love concerneth us to add
Her father's liking; which to bring to pass,
As I before imparted to your worship,
I am to get a man—whatere he be   130
It skills not much, we'll fit him to our turn—
And he shall be Vincentio of Pisa,
And make assurance here in Padua,
Of greater sums than I have promised.
So shall you quietly enjoy your hope,   135
And marry sweet Bianca with consent.
   Lucentio. Were it not that my fellow schoolmaster
Doth watch Bianca's steps so narrowly
'Twere good, methinks, to steal our marriage;
Which once perform'd, let all the world say no,   140
I'll keep mine own despite of all the world.

115 **Good sooth** indeed. **even** read 'e'en.' 117 **wear** wear out.
122 **lovely** loving. 126 **event** outcome; read 'th'event.' 127 **But
to her love** F *But, sir, Love.* 131 **skills** matters. 139 **steal our
marriage** elope.

Tranio. That by degrees we mean to look into
And watch our vantage in this business
We'll overreach the greybeard, Gremio,
The narrow-prying father, Minola,   145
The quaint musician, amorous Licio;
All for my master's sake, Lucentio.

Enter Gremio.

Signior Gremio, came you from the church?
  Gremio. As willingly as ere I came from school.
  Tranio. And is the bride and bridegroom coming
      home?   150
  Gremio. A bridegroom say you? 'Tis a groom in-
      deed,
A grumbling groom, and that the girl shall find.
  Tranio. Curster than she? why, 'tis impossible.
  Gremio. Why, he's a devil, a devil, a very fiend.   154
  Tranio. Why, she's a devil, a devil, the devil's dam.
  Gremio. Tut! she's a lamb, a dove, a fool to him.
I'll tell you, Sir Lucentio: when the priest
Should ask, if Katherine should be his wife,
'Ay, by goggs woones!' quoth he; and swore so loud
That, all amaz'd, the priest let fall the book   160
And, as he stoop'd again to take it up
This mad-brain'd bridegroom took him such a cuff
That down fell priest and book and book and priest.
'Now, take them up,' quoth he, 'if any list.'   164
  Tranio. What said the wench when he rose again?

---

143 **vantage** advantage. **business** three syllables here. 146 **quaint**
artful. **amorous** read 'am'rous.' 151 **groom** i.e. rough as a servingman. 155 **dam** the very mother of the devil; cf. I.3.105. 159
goggs woones corruption of 'God's wounds,' a common oath.
162 **took** dealt. 164 **list** choose to.

Gremio. Trembled and shook; for why, he stamp'd
   and swore,
As if the vicar meant to cozen him.
But after many ceremonies done
He calls for wine: 'A health!' quoth he, as if
He had been aboard, carousing to his mates   170
After a storm; quaff'd off the muscadel
And threw the sops all in the sexton's face,
Having no other reason
But that his beard grew thin and hungerly,
And seem'd to ask him sops as he was drinking.   175
This done, he took the bride about the neck
And kiss'd her lips with such a clamorous smack
That at the parting all the church did echo,
And I, seeing this, came thence for very shame;
And after me, I know, the rout is coming.   180
Such a mad marriage never was before.
Hark, hark! I hear the minstrels play.

                      Music plays.

Enter Petruchio, Katherina, Bianca, Baptista,
   Hortensio [with Grumio and train].

Petruchio. Gentlemen and friends, I thank you for
   your pains.
I know you think to dine with me today   184
And have prepar'd great store of wedding cheer,
But so it is, my haste doth call me hence
And therefore here I mean to take my leave.

166–182 F sets these lines as prose. 167 **cozen** cheat (with invalid
ceremony). 170 **He had** read 'he'd.' **aboard** aboard ship. 171
muscadel sweet wine, commonly drunk at weddings. 172 **sops**
dregs. 174 **hungerly** sparsely. 175 **sops** pieces of cake dipped in
wine. 177 **clamorous** read 'clam'rous.' 180 **rout** mob.

Baptista. Is't possible you will away tonight?

Petruchio. I must away today, before night come.
Make it no wonder; if you knew my business,   190
You would entreat me rather go than stay.
And, honest company, I thank you all,
That have beheld me give away myself
To this most patient, sweet, and virtuous wife.
Dine with my father, drink a health to me,   195
For I must hence; and farewell to you all.

Tranio. Let us entreat you stay till after dinner.

Petruchio. It may not be.

Gremio.   Let me entreat you.

Petruchio. It cannot be.

Katherina.   Let me entreat you.   199

Petruchio. I am content.

Katherina.   Are you content to stay?

Petruchio. I am content you shall entreat me stay,
But yet not stay, entreat me how you can.

Katherina. Now if you love me, stay.

Petruchio.   Grumio, my
     horse!

Grumio. Ay, sir, they be ready; the oats have eaten
     the horses.

Katherina. Nay then,   206
Do what thou canst, I will not go today;
No, nor tomorrow, not till I please myself.
The door is open, sir, there lies your way;
You may be jogging whiles your boots are green;
For me, I'll not be gone till I please myself.   211
'Tis like you'll prove a jolly surly groom,
That take it on you at the first so roundly.

190 **Make it no wonder** do not be surprised. 203 **horse** horses.
210 **green** fresh; proverbial for getting an early start. 212 **jolly**
overbearing. 213 **roundly** unceremoniously.

Petruchio. O Kate! content thee; prethee, be not
  angry.

Katherina. I will be angry; what hast thou to do?
Father, be quiet; he shall stay my leisure.   216

  Gremio. Ay, marry, sir, now it begins to work.

  Katherina. Gentlemen, forward to the bridal dinner:
I see a woman may be made a fool
If she had not a spirit to resist.

  Petruchio. They shall go forward, Kate, at thy
    command.   221
Obey the bride, you that attend on her;
Go to the feast, revel and domineer,
Carouse full measure to her maidenhead,
Be mad and merry, or go hang yourselves;
But for my bonny Kate, she must with me.   226
Nay, look not big, nor stamp, nor stare, nor fret;
I will be master of what is mine own.
She is my goods, my chattels; she is my house,
My household stuff, my field, my barn,
My horse, my ox, my ass, my anything;   231
And here she stands, touch her whoever dare;
I'll bring mine action on the proudest he
That stops my way in Padua. Grumio,
Draw forth thy weapon, we are beset with thieves;
Rescue thy mistress, if thou be a man.   236
Fear not, sweet wench; they shall not touch thee,
    Kate:
I'll buckler thee against a million.

  Exeunt Petruchio, Katherina [and Grumio].

214 prethee prithee, I pray thee; 223 **domineer** carouse. 227 **big**
pompous (addressed to the crowd, not Katherina). 231 **anything**
with allusion to the language of the Tenth Commandment. 233
bring mine action bring a law suit. 238 **buckler** shield.

Baptista. Nay, let them go, a couple of quiet ones.

Gremio. Went they not quickly I should die with
laughing.   240

Tranio. Of all mad matches never was the like.

Lucentio. Mistress, what's your opinion of your
sister?

Bianca. That being mad herself, she's madly mated.

Gremio. I warrant him, Petruchio is Kated.

Baptista. Neighbors and friends, though bride and
bridegroom wants

For to supply the places at the table,   246

You know there wants no junkets at the feast.

Lucentio, you shall supply the bridegroom's place,

And let Bianca take her sister's room.

Tranio. Shall sweet Bianca practice how to bride it?

Baptista. She shall, Lucentio. Come, gentlemen, let's
go.   *Exeunt.*

[SCENE 3]

Enter Grumio.

Grumio. Fie, fie, on all tired jades, on all mad
masters, and all foul ways! Was ever man so beaten?
was ever man so ray'd? was ever man so weary? I
am sent before to make a fire, and they are coming
after to warm them. Now were not I a little pot and
soon hot, my very lips might freeze to my teeth, my
tongue to the roof of my mouth, my heart in my
belly, ere I should come by a fire to thaw me; but I,

245 **wants** are lacking. 247 **junkets** sweetmeats. **Scene 3** N.
3 **ray'd** dirtied. 5 **little pot** proverbial reference to small stature
and quick temper.

66

with blowing the fire, shall warm myself; for, considering the weather, a taller man than I will take cold. Holla, ho! Curtis.   11

Enter Curtis.

Curtis. Who is that calls so coldly?

Grumio. A piece of ice; if thou doubt it, thou mayst slide from my shoulder to my heel with no greater a run but my head and my neck. A fire, good Curtis.

Curtis. Is my master and his wife coming, Grumio?

Grumio. O! ay, Curtis, ay; and therefore fire, fire; cast on no water.   18

Curtis. Is she so hot a shrew as she's reported?

Grumio. She was, good Curtis, before this frost but thou knowest winter tames man, woman, and beast; for it hath tam'd my old master, and my new mistress, and myself, fellow Curtis.   23

Curtis. Away, you three-inch fool! I am no beast.

Grumio. Am I but three inches? why, thy horn is a foot; and so long am I at the least. But wilt thou make a fire or shall I complain on thee to our mistress, whose hand—she being now at hand—thou shalt soon feel, to thy cold comfort, for being slow in thy hot office?   30

Curtis. I prethee, good Grumio, tell me, how goes the world?

Grumio. A cold world, Curtis, in every office but thine; and therefore, fire. Do thy duty, and have thy

10 **taller** with play on the meaning 'finer.' 15 **run** take-off. 24 **I am no beast** Curtis resents being called a fellow of Grumio who has just designated himself 'a beast.' 25 **horn** i.e. as proverbially worn by a cuckold. 30 **office** duty, task.

duty, for my master and mistress are almost frozen
to death.   36

Curtis. There's fire ready; and therefore, good
Grumio, the news?

Grumio. Why, 'Jack, boy! ho, boy!' and as much
news as wilt thou.   40

Curtis. Come, you are so full of cony-catching.

Grumio. Why therefore fire, for I have caught extreme cold. Where's the cook? Is supper ready, the
house trimm'd, rushes strew'd, cobwebs swept; the
servingmen in their new fustian, their white stockings, and every officer his wedding-garment on? Be
the jacks fair within, the jills fair without, the carpets laid and everything in order?   48

Curtis. All ready; and therefore, I pray thee, news?

Grumio. First, know, my horse is tired; my master
and mistress falne out.   51

Curtis. How?

Grumio. Out of their saddles into the dirt—and
thereby hangs a tale.

Curtis. Let's ha't, good Grumio   55

Grumio. Lend thine ear.

Curtis. Here.

Grumio. There.   [*Strikes him.*]

Curtis. This 'tis to feel a tale, not to hear a tale.

---

35 **duty** due, reward (proverbial). 39 **'Jack, boy! ho, boy!'** from
a song (catch) relating the 'news' that the cat is in the well.
41 **cony-catching** evasive tricks, with play on the catch of l. 39.
44 **trimm'd** made trim, orderly. **rushes strew'd** i.e. on the floor.
45 **fustian** coarse cotton cloth. **their** F *the* 46 **officer** servant.
47 **jacks** 1) servingmen, 2) half-pint drinking vessels. **jills** 1)
maidservants, 2) smaller drinking vessels (gills). 47–48 **carpets**
table-covers. 51 **falne** fallen.

Grumio. And therefore 'tis called a sensible tale, and this cuff was but to knock at your ear and beseech listening. Now I begin: *Imprimis*, we came down a foul hill, my master riding behind my mistress—

Curtis. Both of one horse?

Grumio. What's that to thee?   65

Curtis. Why, a horse.

Grumio. Tell thou the tale; but hadst thou not cross'd me thou shouldst have heard how her horse fell and she under her horse; thou shouldst have heard in how miry a place, how she was bemoil'd: how he left her with the horse upon her; how he beat me because her horse stumbled; how she waded through the dirt to pluck him off me: how he swore; how she pray'd, that never pray'd before; how I cried; how the horses ran away; how her bridle was burst; how I lost my crupper; with many things of worthy memory, which now shall die in oblivion, and thou return unexperienc'd to thy grave.   78

Curtis. By this reck'ning he is more shrew than she.

Grumio. Ay; and that, thou and the proudest of you all shall find when he comes home. But what talk I of this? Call forth Nathaniel, Joseph, Nicholas, Philip, Walter, Sugarsop, and the rest; let their heads be slickly comb'd, their blue coats brush'd and their garters of an indifferent knit; let them curtsy with their left legs and not presume to touch a hair of my master's horsetail till they kiss their hands. Are they all ready?   88

Curtis. They are.

60 **sensible** 1) making sense, 2) capable of being felt. 62 **Imprimis** first of all (Latin). 64 **of** on. 70 **bemoil'd** covered with mud. 84 **slickly** smoothly. 85 **indifferent knit** moderately handsome N.

Grumio. Call them forth.   90

Curtis. Do you hear? ho! you must meet my master to countenance my mistress.

Grumio. Why, she hath a face of her own.

Curtis. Who knows not that?   94

Grumio. Thou, it seems, that calls for company to countenance her.

Curtis. I call them forth to credit her.

Grumio. Why, she comes to borrow nothing of them.

Enter four or five Servingmen.

Nathaniel. Welcome home, Grumio!   100

Philip. How now, Grumio?

Joseph. What, Grumio!

Nicholas. Fellow Grumio!

Nathaniel. How now, old lad!   104

Grumio. Welcome, you; how now, you; what, you; fellow, you; and thus much for greeting. Now, my spruce companions, is all ready and all things neat?

Nathaniel. All things is ready. How near is our master?   109

Grumio. E'en at hand, alighted by this; and therefore be not—Cock's passion, silence! I hear my master.

Enter Petruchio and Kate.

Petruchio. Where be these knaves? What! no man at door
To hold my stirrup nor to take my horse?

92 **countenance** do honor to. 96 **countenance** give a face to. 97 **credit** Curtis means 'pay respect to,' Grumio plays with the other meaning 'extend credit.' 111 **Cock's** corruption of 'God's.'

Where is Nathaniel, Gregory, Philip?—   115
  All Servingmen. Here, here, sir; here, sir.
  Petruchio. Here, sir! here, sir! here, sir! here, sir!
You loggerheaded and unpolish'd grooms!
What, no attendance? no regard? no duty?
Where is the foolish knave I sent before?   120
  Grumio. Here, sir; as foolish as I was before.
  Petruchio. You peasant swain! you whoreson malt-
    horse drudge!
Did I not bid thee meet me in the park
And bring along these rascal knaves with thee.   124
  Grumio. Nathaniel's coat, sir, was not fully made
And Gabrel's pumps were all unpink'd i' th' heel;
There was no link to color Peter's hat
And Walter's dagger was not come from sheathing;
There were none fine but Adam, Rafe, and Gregory;
The rest were ragged, old, and beggarly.   130
Yet, as they are, here are they come to meet you.
  Petruchio. Go, rascals, go, and fetch my supper in.
                     Exeunt Servants.
'Where is the life that late I led?'
Where are those—? Sit down, Kate, and welcome.
  Food, food, food, food!

      Enter Servants with supper.

Why, when, I say?—Nay, good sweet Kate, be
  merry.—   136

118 **loggerheaded** blockheaded. 122 **peasant swain** country lout.
whoreson contemptible. **malt-horse drudge** i.e. slow and clumsy
as the horse used to grind malt in a brewery. 126 **unpink'd** with
ornamental embroidery frayed or missing. 127 **link** pitchtorch,
used to give old hats a new blacking. 128 **sheathing** having sheath
made or repaired. 129 **fine** well turned out. 133 '**Where . . . led**'
line of an old song; cf. *2 Henry IV*, V.3.146. 135 **Food . . . food**
F *Soud . . . soud* N.

71

Off with my boots, you rogues! you villains! When?
'It was the friar of orders grey,
As he forth walked on his way':
Out, you rogue! you pluck my foot awry;
Take that, and mend the plucking of the other.   141
                                        [*Strikes him.*]
Be merry, Kate. Some water, here; what, ho!

Enter one with water.

Where's my spaniel Troilus? Sirrah, get you hence
And bid my cousin Ferdinand come hither: 144
                                        [*Exit Servant.*]
One, Kate, that you must kiss and be acquainted
    with.
Where are my slippers? Shall I have some water?
Come, Kate, and wash, and welcome heartily.—
You whoreson villain! will you let it fall?
                                        [*Strikes him.*]
    Katherina. Patience, I pray you; 'twas a fault un-
        willing.   149
    Petruchio. A whoreson, beetle-headed, flap-ear'd
        knave!
Come, Kate, sit down; I know you have a stomach.
Will you give thanks, sweet Kate, or else shall I?—
What's this? mutton?
    1. Servingman.   Ay.
    Petruchio.   Who brought it?
    Peter.   I.
    Petruchio. 'Tis burnt; and so is all the meat.   154
What dogs are these! Where is the rascal cook?
How durst you, villains, bring it from the dresser,

137 **When** exclamation of impatience; cf. *Richard II*, I.1.162.
138–9 'It . . . way' fragment of an old song. 151 **stomach** 1) ap-
petite, 2) temper. 156 **dresser** sideboard.

And serve it thus to me that love it not?

[*Throws the meat about the stage.*]

There, take it to you, trenchers, cups, and all.
You heedless joltheads and unmanner'd slaves!
What, do you grumble? I'll be with you straight.

Katherina. I pray you, husband, be not so disquiet:
The meat was well if you were so contented.   162

Petruchio. I tell thee, Kate, 'twas burnt and dried
      away
And I expressly am forbid to touch it,
For it engenders choler, planteth anger,
And better 'twere that both of us did fast,   166
Since, of ourselves, ourselves are choleric,
Than feed it with such overroasted flesh.
Be patient; tomorrow't shall be mended,
And for this night we'll fast for company.
Come, I will bring thee to thy bridal chamber.   171
                                        Exeunt.

Enter Servants severally.

Nathaniel. Peter, didst ever see the like?
Peter. He kills her in her own humor.

Enter Curtis, a Servant.

Grumio. Where is he?
Curtis. In her chamber, making a sermon of con-
tinency to her;   176
And rails and swears and rates, that she, poor soul,
Knows not which way to stand, to look, to speak,

158 **trenchers** wooden plates. 160 **with you** even with you. **straight**
immediately. 165 **choler** the humor that makes one short-
tempered, choleric. 170 **for** in. 173 **kills . . . humor** subdues her
by employing her own kind of bad temper. SD **Enter Curtis** F
l. 173. 175–179 F sets these lines as prose. 177 **rates** berates. **that**
so that.

And sits as one new-risen from a dream.
Away, away! for he is coming hither.   [*Exeunt.*]

Enter Petruchio.

Petruchio. Thus have I politicly begun my reign
And 'tis my hope to end successfully.   182
My falcon now is sharp and passing empty
And till she stoop she must not be full gorg'd,
For then she never looks upon her lure.
Another way I have to man my haggard,   186
To make her come and know her keeper's call;
That is, to watch her as we watch these kites
That bate and beat and will not be obedient.
She eat no meat today, nor none shall eat;   190
Last night she slept not, nor tonight she shall not:
As with the meat, some undeserved fault
I'll find about the making of the bed
And here I'll fling the pillow, there the bolster,
This way the coverlet, another way the sheets.
Ay, and amid this hurly I intend   196
That all is done in reverend care of her,
And in conclusion she shall watch all night;
And if she chance to nod I'll rail and brawl
And with the clamor keep her still awake.
This is a way to kill a wife with kindness,   201

183 **sharp** . . . **empty** fasting and hence keen for prey. 184 **stoop**
1) swoop (falconry), 2) bow to authority. **full gorg'd** well fed. 185
then i.e. when well fed. **lure** decoy used to recall a falcon N. 186
man tame. **haggard** wild female hawk. 188 **watch** to keep from
sleep. **kites** scavenging birds. 189 **bate and beat** flap and flutter,
words similarly pronounced. 190 **eat** ate. 191 **last night** . . . **shall
not** N. 196 **hurly** commotion. **intend** pretend. 198 **watch** stay
awake. 201 **kill a wife with kindness** N.

And thus I'll curb her mad and headstrong humor.
He that knows better how to tame a shrew,
Now let him speak: 'tis charity to shew.   *Exit.*

[SCENE 4]

Enter Tranio and Hortensio

Tranio. Is't possible, friend Licio, that Mistress
    Bianca
Doth fancy any other but Lucentio?
I tell you, sir, she bears me fair in hand.
    Hortensio. Sir, to satisfy you in what I have said,
Stand by and mark the manner of his teaching.   5
                    [*They stand aside.*]

Enter Bianca [and Lucentio].

Lucentio. Now mistress, profit you in what you
    read?
Bianca. What, master, read you? first resolve me
    that.
Lucentio. I read that I profess, the Art to Love.
Bianca. And may you prove, sir, master of your
    art!
Lucentio. While you, sweet dear, prove mistress of
    my heart.   10
Hortensio. Quick proceeders, marry! Now, tell me,
    I pray,
You that durst swear that your mistress Bianca

202–203 shrew . . . shew both pronounced with *-ow.* 3 **bears
me fair in hand** leads me on. 4–5 F assigns these lines to Lucentio.
6 F assigns this line to Hortensio. 7 **resolve** answer. 8 F assigns
this line to Hortensio. 8–11 N. 11 **marry** a mild oath, originally
to Mary the Virgin.

Lov'd none in the world so well as Lucentio.

Tranio. O despiteful love! unconstant womankind!
I tell thee, Licio, this is wonderful.   15

Hortensio. Mistake no more: I am not Licio,
Nor a musician, as I seem to be;
But one that scorns to live in this disguise,
For such a one as leaves a gentleman
And makes a god of such a cullion.   20
Know, sir, that I am call'd Hortensio.

Tranio. Signior Hortensio, I have often heard
Of your entire affection to Bianca,
And since mine eyes are witness of her lightness
I will with you, if you be so contented,   25
Forswear Bianca and her love forever.

Hortensio. See, how they kiss and court! Signior
    Lucentio,
Here is my hand and here I firmly vow
Never to woo her more, but do forswear her,
As one unworthy all the former favors   30
That I have fondly flatter'd her withal.

Tranio. And here I take the like unfeigned oath,
Never to marry with her though she would entreat.
Fie on her! see how beastly she doth court him.

Hortensio. Would all the world but he had quite
    forsworn!   35
For me, that I may surely keep mine oath,
I will be married to a wealthy widow
Ere three days pass, which hath as long lov'd me
As I have lov'd this proud disdainful haggard.
And so farewell, Signior Lucentio.   40
Kindness in women, not their beauteous looks,
Shall win my love; and so I take my leave

13 **none** F *me.* 18 **scorns** F *scorne.* 20 **cullion** (three syllables
here) low creature. 31 **her** F *them.*

In resolution as I swore before.   *[Exit.]*

  Tranio. Mistress Bianca, bless you with such grace

As longeth to a lover's blessed case!   45

Nay, I have tane you napping, gentle love,

And have forsworn you with Hortensio.

  Bianca. Tranio, you jest. But have you both for-
    sworn me?

  Tranio. Mistress, we have.

  Lucentio.   Then we are rid of Licio.

  Tranio. I' faith, he'll have a lusty widow now,   50

That shall be woo'd and wedded in a day.

  Bianca. God give him joy!

  Tranio. Ay, and he'll tame her.

  Bianca.   He says so, Tranio.

  Tranio. Faith, he is gone unto the taming-school.

  Bianca. The taming-school! what, is there such a
    place?   55

  Tranio. Ay, mistress, and Petruchio is the master,

That teacheth tricks eleven and twenty long

To tame a shrew and charm her chattering tongue.

Enter Biondello.

  Biondello. O master, master! I have watch'd so long

That I'm dog-weary, but at last I spied   60

An ancient angel coming down the hill

Will serve the turn.

  Tranio.   What is he, Biondello?

  Biondello. Master, a marcantant or a pedant—

I know not what; but formal in apparel,

---

45 **longeth** belongeth. 46 **tane** taken. 53 **and** if. 57 **tricks eleven and twenty long** N. 61 **ancient angel** fellow of the old stamp (*angel*, here 'coin'). 62 **Will serve** who will serve. **What** who. 63 **marcantant** Biondello's pronunciation of Italian *mercantante* (merchant).

In gait and countenance surely like a father. 65
  Lucentio. And what of him, Tranio?
  Tranio. If he be credulous and trust my tale
I'll make him glad to seem Vincentio,
And give assurance to Baptista Minola
As if he were the right Vincentio. 70
Take in your love and then let me alone.
                [Exeunt Lucentio and Bianca.]

          Enter a Pedant.

  Pedant. God save you, sir!
  Tranio.   And you, sir! you are
  welcome.
Travel you far on, or are you at the farthest?
  Pedant. Sir, at the farthest for a week or two,
But then up farther and as far as Rome; 75
And so to Tripoli if God lend me life.
  Tranio. What countryman, I pray?
  Pedant.   Of Mantua.
  Tranio. Of Mantua, sir! marry, God forbid!
And come to Padua, careless of your life?
  Pedant. My life, sir! how, I pray? for that goes
  hard. 80
  Tranio. 'Tis death for anyone in Mantua
To come to Padua. Know you not the cause?
Your ships are stay'd at Venice and the duke—
For private quarrel 'twixt your duke and him—
Hath publish'd and proclaim'd it openly. 85
'Tis marvel, but that you are but newly come,
You might have heard it else proclaim'd about.

---

65 **countenance** read 'count'nance.' 71 **Take in** F *Par. Take me.*
80 **goes hard** is serious. 83 **stay'd** detained.
  78

Pedant. Alas, sir! it is worse for me than so,
For I have bills for money by exchange
From Florence and must here deliver them.   90
   Tranio. Well, sir, to do you courtesy,
This will I do and this I will advise you:
First, tell me, have you ever been at Pisa?
   Pedant. Ay, sir, in Pisa have I often bin;
Pisa, renowned for grave citizens.   95
   Tranio. Among them, know you one Vincentio?
   Pedant. I know him not but I have heard of him;
A merchant of incomparable wealth.
   Tranio. He is my father, sir; and, sooth to say,
In count'nance somewhat doth resemble you.   100
   Biondello. [*Aside.*] As much as an apple doth an
oyster, and all one.
   Tranio. To save your life in this extremity
This favor will I do you for his sake,
And think it not the worst of all your fortunes   105
That you are like to Sir Vincentio.
His name and credit shall you undertake
And in my house you shall be friendly lodg'd.
Look that you take upon you as you should!
You understand me, sir; so shall you stay   110
Till you have done your business in the city.
If this be court'sy, sir, accept of it.
   Pedant. O sir, I do; and will repute you ever
The patron of my life and liberty.   114
   Tranio. Then go with me to make the matter good.
This, by the way, I let you understand:
My father is here look'd for every day
To pass assurance of a dower in marriage

102 **all one** no matter. 107 **undertake** assume. 109 **take upon you**
comport yourself. 118 **pass** convey (legal term).

'Twixt me and one Baptista's daughter here.
In all these circumstances I'll instruct you.   120
Go with me to clothe you as becomes you.   *Exeunt*.

120 **circumstances** details.

Act IV

[SCENE 1]

Enter Katherina and Grumio.

Grumio. No, no, forsooth; I dare not for my life.
Katherina. The more my wrong, the more his spite
    appears.
What, did he marry me to famish me?
Beggars, that come unto my father's door,
Upon entreaty have a present alms;   5
If not, elsewhere they meet with charity.
But I, who never knew how to entreat
Nor never needed that I should entreat,
Am starv'd for meat, giddy for lack of sleep,
With oaths kept waking and with brawling fed.   10
And that which spites me more than all these wants,
He does it under name of perfect love,
As who should say, if I should sleep or eat
'Twere deadly sickness or else present death.
I prithee go and get me some repast;   15
I care not what, so it be wholesome food.
  Grumio. What say you to a neat's foot?
  Katherina. 'Tis passing good: I prithee let me have
    it.
  Grumio. I fear it is too choleric a meat.

2 **more** greater. 5 **present** immediate. 13 **As who should say** as
if to say. 17 **neat** ox or calf. 19 **choleric** productive of temper;
cf. III.3.164.

How say you to a fat tripe finely broil'd?   20
  Katherina. I like it well: good Grumio, fetch it me.
  Grumio. I cannot tell; I fear 'tis choleric.
What say you to a piece of beef and mustard?
  Katherina. A dish that I do love to feed upon.
  Grumio. Ay, but the mustard is too hot a little. 25
  Katherina. Why then, the beef, and let the mustard
    rest.
  Grumio. Nay then, I will not; you shall have the
    mustard
Or else you get no beef of Grumio.   28
  Katherina. Then both or one, or anything thou wilt.
  Grumio. Why then, the mustard without the beef.
  Katherina. Go, get thee gone, thou false deluding
    slave,   *Beats him.*
That feed'st me with the very name of meat.
Sorrow on thee and all the pack of you
That triumph thus upon my misery!
Go, get thee gone, I say.   35

Enter Petruchio, and Hortensio with meat.

  Petruchio. How fares my Kate? What, sweeting,
    all amort?
  Hortensio. Mistress, what cheer?
  Katherina.   Faith, as cold as
    can be.
  Petruchio. Pluck up thy spirits; look cheerfully
    upon me.
Here, love; thou seest how diligent I am
To dress thy meat myself and bring it thee.   40
I am sure, sweet Kate, this kindness merits thanks.
What! not a word? Nay then, thou lov'st it not

36 **all amort** out of spirits.

And all my pains is sorted to no proof.
Here, take away this dish.
 Katherina.   I pray you, let it stand.
 Petruchio. The poorest service is repaid with thanks
And so shall mine, before you touch the meat. 46
 Katherina. I thank you, sir.
 Hortensio. Signior Petruchio, fie! you are to blame.
Come, Mistress Kate, I'll bear you company.
 Petruchio. Eat it up all, Hortensio, if thou lov'st
  me. 50
Much good do it unto thy gentle heart!
Kate, eat apace. And now, my honey love,
Will we return unto thy father's house
And revel it as bravely as the best,
With silken coats and caps and golden rings, 55
With ruffs and cuffs and fardingales and things;
With scarfs and fans and double change of brav'ry,
With amber bracelets, beads, and all this knav'ry.
What! hast thou din'd? The tailor stays thy leisure
To deck thy body with his ruffling treasure. 60

Enter Tailor.

Come, tailor, let us see these ornaments;
Lay forth the gown.—

Enter Haberdasher.

       What news with you, sir?
 Haberdasher. Here is the cap your worship did bespeak.

---

43 **sorted to no proof** attended by no corresponding result; fruit-
less. 54 **bravely** finely dressed. 56 **fardingales** hoopskirts. 57
bravery finery. 58 **knavery** coquettish adornment. 59 **stays** awaits.
60 **ruffling** ornamented with ruffles. SD **Haberdasher** F *Fel.* 63
bespeak order.

Petruchio. Why, this was molded on a porringer;
A velvet dish: fie, fie! 'tis lewd and filthy: 65
Why, 'tis a cockle or a walnut shell,
A knack, a toy, a trick, a baby's cap—
Away with it! come, let me have a bigger.
  Katherina. I'll have no bigger, this doth fit the time
And gentlewomen wear such caps as these. 70
  Petruchio. When you are gentle you shall have one too—
And not till then.
  Hortensio. [*Aside.*] That will not be in haste
  Katherina. Why, sir, I trust I may have leave to speak,
And speak I will; I am no child, no babe.
Your betters have endur'd me say my mind 75
And if you cannot, best you stop your ears.
My tongue will tell the anger of my heart,
Or else my heart, concealing it, will break,
And rather than it shall I will be free
Even to the uttermost, as I please, in words. 80
  Petruchio. Why, thou sayst true; it is a paltry cap,
A custard-coffin, a bauble, a silken pie.
I love thee well in that thou lik'st it not.
  Katherina. Love me or love me not, I like the cap
And it I will have or I will have none. 85

                                  Exit Haberdasher.

  Petruchio. Thy gown? why, ay: come, tailor, let us see't.
O mercy, God! what masquing stuff is here?

---

65 **lewd** vile. 66 **cockle** sea shell. 67 **knack** knickknack. **trick** trifle.
69 **fit the time** suit the present fashion. 82 **custard-coffin** raised
crust of pastry. **pie** shaped like a meat pie, i.e. circular and five
or six inches high. 87 **masquing** fit only for masquerade.

What's this? a sleeve? 'tis like a demi-cannon.
What! up and down, carv'd like an apple tart?
Here's snip and nip and cut and slish and slash,   90
Like to a censer in a barber's shop.
Why, what, a devil's name, tailor, call'st thou this?
  Hortensio. [*Aside.*] I see, she's like to have neither
    cap nor gown.
  Tailor. You bid me make it orderly and well,
According to the fashion and the time.   95
  Petruchio. Marry, and did; but if you be remem-
    b'red,
I did not bid you mar it to the time.
Go, hop me over every kennel home,
For you shall hop without my custom, sir.
I'll none of it: hence! make your best of it.   100
  Katherina. I never saw a better-fashion'd gown,
More quaint, more pleasing, nor more commendable.
Belike you mean to make a puppet of me.
  Petruchio. Why, true; he means to make a puppet
    of thee.
  Tailor. She says your worship means to make a
    puppet of her.   105
  Petruchio. O monstrous arrogance!
Thou liest, thou thread, thou thimble,
Thou yard, three-quarters, half yard, quarter, nail!
Thou flea, thou nit, thou winter-cricket thou!   109
Brav'd in mine own house with a skein of thread!
Away! thou rag, thou quantity, thou remnant,

88 **demi-cannon** kind of large cannon. 91 **censer** brazier with per-
forated cover, used by barbers to burn perfumes and thus sweeten
air of the shop. 93 **to have** read 't'have.' 96 **did** I did. **be remem-
b'red** remember. 98 **kennel** gutter. 102 **quaint** pretty. 108 **nail**
measure of two and a quarter inches. 109 **nit** egg of a louse.
110 **Brav'd** defied. **with** by. 111 **quantity** small fragment.

Or I shall so bemete thee with thy yard
As thou shalt think on prating whilst thou liv'st!
I tell thee, I, that thou hast marr'd her gown.   114

  Tailor. Your worship is deceiv'd; the gown is made
Just as my master had direction.
Grumio gave order how it should be done.

  Grumio. I gave him no order; I gave him the stuff.

  Tailor. But how did you desire it should be made?

  Grumio. Marry, sir, with needle and thread.   120

  Tailor. But did you not request to have it cut?

  Grumio. Thou hast fac'd many things.

  Tailor. I have.

  Grumio. Face not me: thou hast brav'd many men;
brave not me: I will neither be fac'd nor brav'd. I
say unto thee, I bid thy master cut out the gown
but I did not bid him cut it to pieces; *ergo*, thou
liest.

  Tailor. Why, here is the note of the fashion to
testify.   130

  Petruchio. Read it.

  Grumio. The note lies in's throat if he say I said so.

  Tailor. 'Imprimis, a loose-bodied gown.'

  Grumio. Master, if ever I said loose-bodied gown,
sew me in the skirts of it and beat me to death with
a bottom of brown thread. I said, a gown.   136

  Petruchio. Proceed.

  Tailor. 'With a small compass'd cape.'

  Grumio. I confess the cape.

---

112 **bemete** measure. 113 **think on prating** remember your idle
talk. 122 **fac'd** trimmed. 124 **face** affront. **brav'd** dressed in
finery. 125 **brave** defy. 127 **ergo** therefore (Latin). 136 **bottom**
ball. 138 **compass'd** i.e. with the edge forming a circle.

Tailor. 'With a trunk sleeve.'   140

Grumio. I confess two sleeves.

Tailor. 'The sleeves curiously cut.'

Petruchio. Ay, there's the villainy.

Grumio. Error i' th' bill, sir; error i' th' bill. I
commanded the sleeves should be cut out and sewed
up again and that I'll prove upon thee, though thy
little finger be armed in a thimble.

Tailor. This is true that I say; and I had thee in
place where, thou shouldst know it.   149

Grumio. I am for thee straight. Take thou the bill,
give me thy mete-yard, and spare not me.

Hortensio. God-a-mercy, Grumio! then he shall have
no odds.

Petruchio. Well, sir, in brief, the gown is not for me.

Grumio. You are i' th' right, sir; 'tis for my mistress.   156

Petruchio. Go, take it up unto thy master's use.

Grumio. Villain, not for thy life! take up my mistress' gown for thy master's use!

Petruchio. Why sir, what's your conceit in that?

Grumio. O sir, the conceit is deeper than you think
for.   161
Take up my mistress' gown to his master's use!
O, fie, fie, fie!

Petruchio. [*Aside.*] Hortensio, say thou wilt see the
tailor paid.
Go take it hence; be gone and say no more.   165

---

140 **trunk sleeve** very full sleeve; cf. l. 88 above. 142 **curiously**
carefully. 148 **and** and if. 148–9 **in place where** in a suitable place.
150 **bill** with pun on usual meaning and the sense of 'halberd.'
151 **mete-yard** yardstick. 157 **unto thy master's use** i.e. for
whatever purpose he can find for it. 161 **conceit** meaning.

Hortensio. Tailor, I'll pay thee for thy gown to-
    morrow;
Take no unkindness of his hasty words.
Away! I say; commend me to thy master.

                       Exit Tailor.

  Petruchio. Well, come, my Kate; we will unto your
    father's,
Even in these honest mean habiliments.   170
Our purses shall be proud, our garments poor,
For 'tis the mind that makes the body rich;
And as the sun breaks through the darkest clouds
So honor peereth in the meanest habit.
What, is the jay more precious than the lark   175
Because his feathers are more beautiful?
Or is the adder better than the eel
Because his painted skin contents the eye?
O no, good Kate; neither art thou the worse
For this poor furniture and mean array.   180
If thou account'st it shame, lay it on me.
And therefore frolic; we will hence forthwith
To feast and sport us at thy father's house.
Go call my men, and let us straight to him;
And bring our horses unto Long-lane end;   185
There will we mount, and thither walk on foot.
Let's see; I think 'tis now some seven o'clock
And well we may come there by dinnertime.
  Katherina. I dare assure you, sir, 'tis almost two
And 'twill be suppertime ere you come there.   190
  Petruchio. It shall be seven ere I go to horse.
Look, what I speak or do or think to do,
You are still crossing it. Sirs, let't alone:
I will not go today; and ere I do,

174 **peereth** appears. **habit** dress. 180 **furniture** adornment, costume. 181 **account'st** F *accountedst.*

It shall be what o'clock I say it is.   195
  Hortensio. Why, so this gallant will command the
    sun.   *Exeunt.*

[SCENE 2]

Enter Tranio, and the Pedant dressed like Vincentio.

  Tranio. Sir, this is the house: please it you that I
    call?
  Pedant. Ay, what else? and, but I be deceived,
Signior Baptista may remember me,
Near twenty years ago, in Genoa,
Where we were lodgers at the Pegasus.   5
  Tranio. 'Tis well; and hold your own in any case
With such austerity as longeth to a father.
  Pedant. I warrant you. But sir, here comes your
    boy;
'Twere good he were school'd.

Enter Biondello.

  Tranio. Fear you not him. Sirrah Biondello,   10
Now do your duty throughly, I advise you:
Imagine 'twere the right Vincentio.
  Biondello. Tut! fear not me.
  Tranio. But hast thou done thy errand to Baptista?
  Biondello. I told him that your father was at
    Venice,   15
And that you look'd for him this day in Padua.
  Tranio. Th' art a tall fellow: hold thee that to
    drink.

1 **Sir** F *Sirs.* **this is** read 'this.' 5 F assigns this line to Tranio.
Pegasus common name for an inn. 7 **longeth** belongs. 11 **throughly**
thoroughly. 17 **tall** clever. **hold** take (Tranio tips him).

Here comes Baptista. Set your countenance, sir.

Enter Baptista and Lucentio.

Signior Baptista, you are happily met.
[*To the Pedant.*] Sir, this is the gentleman I told
    you of.   20
I pray you, stand good father to me now,
Give me Bianca for my patrimony.
  Pedant. Soft, son!
Sir, by your leave: having come to Padua
To gather in some debts, my son Lucentio   25
Made me acquainted with a weighty cause
Of love between your daughter and himself.
And—for the good report I hear of you,
And for the love he beareth to your daughter,
And she to him—to stay him not too long,   30
I am content, in a good father's care,
To have him match'd; and if you please to like
No worse than I, upon some agreement
Me shall you find ready and willing
With one consent to have her so bestow'd;   35
For curious I cannot be with you,
Signior Baptista, of whom I hear so well.
  Baptista. Sir, pardon me in what I have to say:
Your plainness and your shortness please me well.
Right true it is, your son Lucentio here   40
Doth love my daughter and she loveth him—
Or both dissemble deeply their affections—
And therefore, if you say no more than this,
That like a father you will deal with him
And pass my daughter a sufficient dower,   45

18 **countenance** read 'count'nance.' SD F adds *Pedant booted and
bare-headed* N. 20 this is read 'this.' 23–4 **Soft . . . Padua** F sets
as one line. 36 **curious** cautious.
    90

The match is made; and all is done;
Your son shall have my daughter with consent.
  Tranio. I thank you, sir. Where then, do you know best
We be affied and such assurance tane
As shall with either part's agreement stand?   50
  Baptista. Not in my house, Lucentio; for, you know,
Pitchers have ears, and I have many servants.
Besides, old Gremio is heark'ning still,
And happily we might be interrupted.
  Tranio. Then at my lodging and it like you: 55
There doth my father lie, and there this night
We'll pass the business privately and well.
Send for your daughter by your servant here;
My boy shall fetch the scrivener presently.
The worst is this, that, at so slender warning,   60
You are like to have a thin and slender pittance.
  Baptista. It likes me well. Cambio, hie you home
And bid Bianca make her ready straight;
And, if you will, tell what hath happened:
Lucentio's father is arriv'd in Padua,   65
And how she's like to be Lucentio's wife.
  Lucentio. I pray the gods she may with' all my heart!   *Exit Lucentio.*
  Tranio. Dally not with the gods, but get thee gone.
Signior Baptista, shall I lead the way?
Welcome! one mess is like to be your cheer.   70

---

49 **affied** formally betrothed. 53 **heark'ning still** always listening.
54 **happily** perhaps. 55 **and it like** if it please. 56 **lie** lodge. 57 **pass**
transact. 59 **scrivener** notary; read 'scriv'ner.' 61 **pittance** meal.
62 **likes** pleases. 66 **like** likely. 67 F assigns this line to Biondello N.
68 F adds SD *Enter Peter* N. 70 **mess** dish. **cheer** entertainment.

Come, sir ; we will better it in Pisa.

Baptista. I follow you.   *Exeunt.*

Enter Lucentio and Biondello.

Biondello. Cambio !

Lucentio. What sayst thou, Biondello?   74

Biondello. You saw my master wink and laugh upon you?

Lucentio. Biondello, what of that?

Biondello. Faith, nothing; but has left me here behind to expound the meaning or moral of his signs and tokens.   80

Lucentio. I pray thee, moralize them.

Biondello. Then thus. Baptista is safe, talking with the deceiving father of a deceitful son.

Lucentio. And what of him?   84

Biondello. His daughter is to be brought by you to the supper.

Lucentio. And then?

Biondello. The old priest at Saint Luke's church is at your command at all hours.

Lucentio. And what of all this?   90

Biondello. I cannot tell, except they are busied about a counterfeit assurance: take you assurance of her, *cum previlegio ad impremendum solem.* To th' church ! take the priest, clark, and some sufficient honest witnesses.   95

If this be not that you look for, I have no more to say,

But bid Bianca farewell forever and a day.

Lucentio. Hear'st thou, Biondello?   98

Biondello. I cannot tarry: I knew a wench married

78 **has** he has. 81 **moralize** explain. 91 **except** F *expect.* 92 **assurance** betrothal. 93 **cum . . . solem** N.

92

in an afternoon as she went to the garden for parsley to stuff a rabbit; and so may you, sir; and so, adieu, sir. My master hath appointed me to go to Saint Luke's, to bid the priest be ready to come against you come with your appendix.　　　　　*Exit.*

Lucentio. I may, and will, if she be so contented.
She will be pleas'd; then wherefore should I doubt?
Hap what hap may, I'll roundly go about her;　107
It shall go hard if Cambio go without her.　　*Exit.*

[SCENE 3]

Enter Petruchio, Katherina, Hortensio
[with Servants.]

Petruchio. Come on, a God's name; once more to-
　　ward our father's.
Good Lord, how bright and goodly shines the moon!
　Katherina. The moon! the sun: it is not moonlight
　　now.　　　　　　　　　　　　　　　　　3
　Petruchio. I say it is the moon that shines so bright.
　Katherina. I know it is the sun that shines so bright.
　Petruchio. Now, by my mother's son, and that's
　　myself,
It shall be moon or star or what I list,
Or ere I journey to your father's house.
Go on and fetch our horses back again.　　　9
Evermore cross'd and cross'd; nothing but cross'd!
　Hortensio. Say as he says or we shall never go.
　Katherina. Forward, I pray, since we have come so
　　far,

103 **against** by the time that. 104 **appendix** addition or adjunct, here 'wife.' 1 **a** in. 8 **Or ere** before.

And be it moon or sun or what you please.
And if you please to call it a rush-candle,
Henceforth I vow it shall be so for me.   15
  Petruchio. I say it is the moon.
  Katherina.   I know it is the
    moon.
  Petruchio. Nay, then you lie; it is the blessed sun.
  Katherina. Then God be bless'd, it is the blessed
    sun!
But sun it is not when you say it is not,
And the moon changes even as your mind.   20
What you will have it nam'd, even that it is;
And so it shall be so for Katherine.
  Hortensio. Petruchio, go thy ways; the field is won.
  Petruchio. Well, forward, forward! thus the bowl
    should run
And not unluckily against the bias.   25
But soft! company is coming here.

Enter Vincentio.

[*To Vincentio.*] Good morrow, gentle mistress: where
    away?
Tell me, sweet Kate, and tell me truly too,
Hast thou beheld a fresher gentlewoman?
Such war of white and red within her cheeks!   30
What stars do spangle heaven with such beauty
As those two eyes become that heavenly face?
Fair lovely maid, once more good day to thee.
Sweet Kate, embrace her for her beauty's sake.
  Hortensio. A will make the man mad, to make a
    woman of him.   36

14 **rush-candle** rush, dipped in grease to serve as candle. 18 **is** F
in. 24 **bowl** wooden ball used in game of bowls. 25 **bias** N. 35 **A**
he.

Lucentio. I fly, Biondello, but they may chance to
need thee at home; therefore leave us.   4
                              Exit [with Bianca].
Biondello. Nay, faith, I'll see the church a your
back; and then come back to my master's as soon as
I can.   *[Exit.]*
Gremio. I marvel Cambio comes not all this while.

*Enter Petruchio, Kate, Vincentio, [and] Grumio
with Attendants.*

Petruchio. Sir, here's the door, this is Lucentio's
      house:
My father's bears more toward the market place; 10
Thither must I and here I leave you, sir.
Vincentio. You shall not choose but drink before
      you go.
I think I shall command your welcome here
And, by all likelihood, some cheer is toward. *Knock.*
Gremio. They're busy within; you were best knock
louder.   16

Pedant looks out of the window.

Pedant. What's he that knocks as he would beat
down the gate?
Vincentio. Is Signior Lucentio within, sir?
Pedant. He's within, sir, but not to be spoken
withal.   21
Vincentio. What if a man bring him a hundred
pound or two, to make merry withal?
Pedant. Keep your hundred pounds to yourself; he
shall need none so long as I live.   25

---

5 **a your back** on your back; I'll see you into the church. 6 **master's**
F *mistris*. 10 **bears** stands. 17 **What's he** who is he. 21 **withal** with.

Petruchio. Nay, I told you your son was well beloved in Padua. Do you hear, sir? To leave frivolous
circumstances, I pray you tell Signior Lucentio that
his father is come from Pisa and is here at the door
to speak with him.   30

Pedant. Thou liest; his father is come from Padua
and here looking out at the window.

Vincentio. Art thou his father?

Pedant. Ay sir, so his mother says, if I may believe
her.   35

Petruchio. [*To Vincentio.*] Why how now, gentleman! why this is flat knavery, to take upon you
another man's name.

Pedant. Lay hands on the villain; I believe, a means
to cozen somebody in this city under my countenance.

Enter Biondello.

Biondello. I have seen them in the church together;
God send 'em good shipping! But who is here? mine
old master, Vincentio! now we are undone and
brought to nothing.

Vincentio. Come hither, crack-hemp.   45

Biondello. I hope I may choose, sir.

Vincentio. Come hither, you rogue. What, have you
forgot me?

Biondello. Forgot you! no sir. I could not forget
you, for I never saw you before in all my life.   50

Vincentio. What, you notorious villain! didst thou
never see thy master's father, Vincentio?

Biondello. What, my old, worshipful old master?

27–8 **frivolous circumstances** unimportant details. 37 **flat** down-
right. 39 **a** he. 42 **good shipping** i.e. 'fair sailing.' 45 **crack-hemp**
gallows bird. 46 **I . . . sir** Allow me, sir! N. 52 **master's** F
Mistris.

98

yes, marry, sir : see where he looks out of the window.

Vincentio. Is't so, indeed?   *He beats Biondello.*

Biondello. Help, help, help! here's a madman will murder me.   [*Exit.*]

Pedant. Help, son! help, Signior Baptista!

                   [*Exit from above.*]

Petruchio. Prithee, Kate, let's stand aside and see the end of this controversy.   60

                   [*They retire.*]

Enter Pedant [below] with Servants, Baptista,
[and] Tranio.

Tranio. Sir, what are you that offer to beat my servant?   62

Vincentio. What am I, sir! nay, what are you, sir? O immortal gods! O fine villain! A silken doublet! a velvet hose! a scarlet cloak! and a copatain hat! O, I am undone! I am undone! while I play the good husband at home, my son and my servant spend all at the university.

Tranio. How now! what's the matter?

Baptista. What, is the man lunatic?   70

Tranio. Sir, you seem a sober ancient gentleman by your habit, but your words show you a madman. Why sir, what cerns it you if I wear pearl and gold? I thank my good father, I am able to maintain it.

Vincentio. Thy father! O villain! he is a sailmaker in Bergamo.   76

Baptista. You mistake, sir, you mistake, sir. Pray, what do you think is his name?

Vincentio. His name! as if I knew not his name! I

59 **Prithee** F *Preethe.* 65 **copatain hat** high sugar-loaf hat. 67 **husband** frugal manager. 72 **habit** outward semblance. 73 **cerns** concerns.

have brought him up ever since he was three years
old, and his name is Tranio.   81

Pedant. Away, away, mad ass! his name is Lucentio
and he is mine only son, and heir to the lands of me,
Signior Vincentio.

Vincentio. Lucentio! O he hath murd'red his master.
Lay hold on him, I charge you in the duke's name.
O my son, my son! tell me, thou villain, where is my
son Lucentio?

Tranio. Call forth an officer.   89

[*Enter one with an Officer.*]

Carry this mad knave to the jail. Father Baptista,
I charge you see that he be forthcoming.

Vincentio. Carry me to the jail!

Gremio. Stay, officer: he shall not go to prison.

Baptista. Talk not, Signior Gremio. I say he shall
go to prison.   95

Gremio. Take heed, Signior Baptista, lest you be
cony-catched in this business. I dare swear this is the
right Vincentio.

Pedant. Swear, if thou dar'st.

Gremio. Nay, I dare not swear it.   100

Tranio. Then thou wert best say that I am not
Lucentio.

Gremio. Yes, I know thee to be Signior Lucentio.

Baptista. Away with the dotard; to the jail with
him!   105

Vincentio. Thus strangers may be hal'd and abused;
O monstrous villain!

Enter Biondello, Lucentio, and Bianca.

97 cony-catched duped.
   100

Biondello. O we are spoil'd; and yonder he is: deny him, forswear him, or else we are all undone.   109

> *Exeunt Biondello, Tranio, and Pedant as fast as may be.*

Lucentio. Pardon, sweet father.   *Kneel.*
Vincentio.   Lives my sweet son?
Bianca. Pardon, dear father.
Baptista.   How hast thou
     offended?
Where is Lucentio?
Lucentio.   Here's Lucentio,
Right son to the right Vincentio,
That have by marriage made thy daughter mine
While counterfeit supposes blear'd thine eyne.   115
Gremio. Here's packing, with a witness, to deceive
us all!
Vincentio. Where is that damned villain Tranio
That fac'd and brav'd me in this matter so?
Baptista. Why, tell me, is not this my Cambio?   120
Bianca. Cambio is chang'd into Lucentio.
Lucentio. Love wrought these miracles. Bianca's
     love
Made me exchange my state with Tranio
While he did bear my countenance in the town,
And happily I have arriv'd at the last   125
Unto the wished haven of my bliss.
What Tranio did, myself enforc'd him to;
Then pardon him, sweet father, for my sake.
Vincentio. I'll slit the villain's nose, that would have
sent me to the jail.   130

SD **Exeunt** F *Exit.* 115 **supposes** substitutions, probably with
allusion to Gascoigne's play; see Appendix B. **eyne** eyes. 116
packing plotting. **with a witness** with a vengeance. 124 **countenance** read 'count'nance.'

Baptista. But do you hear, sir? Have you married my daughter without asking my good will?   132

Vincentio. Fear not, Baptista; we will content you, go to: but I will in, to be reveng'd for this villainy.
                                                        Exit.

Baptista. And I, to sound the depth of this knavery.
                                                        Exit.

Lucentio. Look not pale, Bianca; thy father will not frown.   *Exeunt [Lucentio and Bianca].*

Gremio. My cake is dough, but I'll in among the rest

Out of hope of all but my share of the feast. [*Exit.*]

Katherina. Husband, let's follow, to see the end of this ado.   141

Petruchio. First kiss me, Kate, and we will.

Katherina. What! in the midst of the street?

Petruchio. What! art thou asham'd of me?

Katherina. No sir, God forbid; but asham'd to kiss.

Petruchio. Why, then let's home again. Come sirrah, let's away.   146

Katherina. Nay, I will give thee a kiss; now pray thee, love, stay.

Petruchio. Is not this well? Come, my sweet Kate; Better once than never, for never too late.   *Exeunt.*

---

134 **go to** expression of remonstrance (or, sometimes, impatience). 138 **My cake is dough** proverbial for failure of an enterprise; cf. I.3.108–109. 141 **ado** commotion. 149 **Better . . . late** i.e. 'better late than never.'

Act V

[SCENE 1]

*Enter Baptista, Vincentio, Gremio, the Pedant,
Lucentio, and Bianca, Tranio, Biondello, Grumio,
[Petruchio, Katherina, Hortensio,] and Widow;
the Servingmen with Tranio bringing in a banquet.*

Lucentio. At last, though long, our jarring notes
        agree;
And time it is, when raging war is done,
To smile at scapes and perils overblown.
My fair Bianca, bid my father welcome
While I with self-same kindness welcome thine.   5
Brother Petruchio, sister Katherina,
And thou, Hortensio, with thy loving widow,
Feast with the best and welcome to my house;
My banket is to close our stomachs up
After our great good cheer. Pray you, sit down;   10
For now we sit to chat as well as eat.
        Petruchio. Nothing but sit and sit, and eat and eat!
        Baptista. Padua affords this kindness, son Pe-
        truchio.
        Petruchio. Padua affords nothing but what is kind.
        Hortensio. For both our sakes I would that word
        were true.   15

SD **banquet** dessert; spelled *banket* l. 9. **1 long** after a long time.
2 done F *come.* **9 stomachs** with second sense of 'quarrel.'

Petruchio. Now, for my life, Hortensio fears his
    widow.

Widow. Then never trust me, if I be afeard.

Petruchio. You are very sensible and yet you miss
    my sense:

I mean, Hortensio is afeard of you.

Widow. He that is giddy thinks the world turns
    round.   20

Petruchio. Roundly replied.

Katherina.   Mistress, how mean you
    that?

Widow. Thus I conceive by him.

Petruchio. Conceives by me! How likes Hortensio
    that?

Hortensio. My widow says, thus she conceives her
    tale.

Petruchio. Very well mended. Kiss him for that,
    good widow.   25

Katherina. 'He that is giddy thinks the world turns
    round':

I pray you, tell me what you meant by that.

Widow. Your husband, being troubled with a shrew,

Measures my husband's sorrow by his woe,

And now you know my meaning.   30

Katherina. A very mean meaning.

Widow.   Right, I mean
    you.

Katherina. And I am mean indeed, respecting you.

Petruchio. To her, Kate!

Hortensio. To her, widow!

---

16 **fears** used by Petruchio in current sense; the widow takes it
in the sense of 'frighten.' 17 **afeard** suspicious. 21 **Roundly**
frankly. 22 **Thus I conceive by him** that is my impression of his
state. Petruchio plays on the other meaning in his reply.

Petruchio. A hundred marks, my Kate does put her
    down.   35

Hortensio. That's my office.

Petruchio. Spoke like an officer; ha' to thee, lad.
                              Drinks to Hortensio.

Baptista. How likes Gremio these quick-witted
    folks?

Gremio. Believe me, sir, they butt together well.

Bianca. Head and butt! an hasty-witted body   40
Would say your head and butt were head and horn.

Vincentio. Ay, mistress bride, hath that awaken'd
    you?

Bianca. Ay, but not frighted me; therefore I'll sleep
    again.

Petruchio. Nay, that you shall not; since you have
    begun,
Have at you for a bitter jest or two.   45

Bianca. Am I your bird? I mean to shift my bush;
And then pursue me as you draw your bow.
You are welcome all.
            Exit Bianca [with Katherina and Widow].

Petruchio. She hath prevented me. Here, Signior
    Tranio;
This bird you aim'd at, though you hit her not: 50
Therefore a health to all that shot and miss'd.

Tranio. O sir! Lucentio slipp'd me, like his grey-
    hound,
Which runs himself and catches for his master.

Petruchio. A good swift simile but something cur-
    rish.   54

---

37 **ha' to** here's to. 45 **Have at you** here goes. **bitter** sharp; F
better. 46 **bird** in the sense of a target. 49 **prevented** anticipated.
52 **slipp'd** unleashed.

Tranio. 'Tis well, sir, that you hunted for yourself;
'Tis thought your deer does hold you at a bay.

Baptista. O ho, Petruchio! Tranio hits you now.

Lucentio. I thank thee for that gird, good Tranio.

Hortensio. Confess, confess, hath he not hit you
here?

Petruchio. A has a little gall'd me, I confess;   60
And, as the jest did glance away from me,
'Tis ten to one it maim'd you two outright.

Baptista. Now, in good sadness, son Petruchio,
I think thou hast the veriest shrew of all.

Petruchio. Well, I say no: and therefore, for assur-
ance,   65
Let's each one send unto his wife,
And he whose wife is most obedient
To come at first when he doth send for her
Shall win the wager which we will propose.

Hortensio. Content. What's the wager?

Lucentio.   Twenty
crowns.   70

Petruchio. Twenty crowns!
I'll venture so much of my hawk or hound,
But twenty times so much upon my wife.

Lucentio. A hundred then.

Hortensio.   Content.

Petruchio.   A match! 'tis
done.

Hortensio. Who shall begin?

Lucentio.   That will I.   75
Go Biondello, bid your mistress come to me.

---

56 **deer** with a pun on 'dear.' **at a bay** at bay. 58 **gird** taunt. 60 **A**
he. **gall'd** scratched. 63 **good sadness** all seriousness. 65 **for assurance** to make sure. **for** F *sir.* 72 **of** on. 74 **A match** i.e. it's a bet.

Biondello. I go. *Exit.*

Baptista. Son, I'll be your half, Bianca comes.

Lucentio. I'll have no halves; I'll bear it all myself.

Enter Biondello.

How now! what news?

Biondello. Sir, my mistress sends you
word 80

That she is busy and she cannot come.

Petruchio. How! she is busy and she cannot come!

Is that an answer?

Gremio. Ay, and a kind one too;

Pray God, sir, your wife send you not a worse.

Petruchio. I hope, better. 85

Hortensio. Sirrah Biondello, go and entreat my
wife

To come to me forthwith. *Exit Biondello.*

Petruchio. O ho! entreat her!

Nay, then she must needs come.

Hortensio. I am afraid, sir,

Do what you can, yours will not be entreated.

Enter Biondello.

Now where's my wife? 90

Biondello. She says you have some goodly jest in
hand.

She will not come; she bids you come to her.

Petruchio. Worse and worse; she will not come! O
vilde,

Intolerable, not to be endur'd!

Sirrah Grumio, go to your mistress; say 95

I command her come to me. *Exit* [*Grumio*].

78 **be your half** take half of your bet. 93 **vilde** vile.

Hortensio.   I know her answer.

Petruchio. What?

Hortensio. She will not.

Petruchio. The fouler fortune mine, and there an end.

Enter Katherina.

Baptista. Now, by my hollidam, here comes Katherina!   100

Katherina. What is your will, sir, that you send for me?

Petruchio. Where is your sister, and Hortensio's wife?

Katherina. They sit conferring by the parlor fire.

Petruchio. Go fetch them hither; if they deny to come,   104

Swinge me them soundly forth unto their husbands.

Away, I say, and bring them hither straight.

                           [Exit Katherina.]

Lucentio. Here is a wonder, if you talk of a wonder.

Hortensio. And so it is. I wonder what it bodes.

Petruchio. Marry, peace it bodes, and love, and quiet life,

An awful rule and right supremacy;   110

And, to be short, what not that's sweet and happy.

Baptista. Now fair befall thee, good Petruchio!

The wager thou hast won and I will add

Unto their losses twenty thousand crowns,

Another dowry to another daughter,   115

For she is chang'd, as she had never been.

Petruchio. Nay, I will win my wager better yet

100 **hollidam** halidom (salvation). 104 **deny** refuse. 105 **Swinge** whip. 110 **awful rule** order commanding respect. 112 **fair befall thee** good luck to you.

And show more sign of her obedience,
Her new-built virtue and obedience.   119

    Enter Kate, Bianca, and Widow.

See where she comes and brings your froward wives
As prisoners to her womanly persuasion.
Katerine, that cap of yours becomes you not:
Off with that bauble, throw it under foot.
  Widow. Lord! let me never have a cause to sigh
Till I be brought to such a silly pass!   125
  Bianca. Fie! what a foolish duty call you this?
  Lucentio. I would your duty were as foolish too;
The wisdom of your duty, fair Bianca,
Hath cost me five hundred crowns since suppertime.
  Bianca. The more fool you for laying on my duty.
  Petruchio. Katherine, I charge thee, tell these head-
    strong women   131
What duty they do owe their lords and husbands.
  Widow. Come, come, you're mocking; we will have
    no telling.
  Petruchio. Come on, I say; and first begin with her.
  Widow. She shall not.   135
  Petruchio. I say she shall: and first begin with her.
  Katherina. Fie, fie! unknit that threat'ning unkind
    brow
And dart not scornful glances from those eyes
To wound thy lord, thy king, thy governor.
It blots thy beauty as frosts do bite the meads,   140
Confounds thy fame as whirlwinds shake fair buds,
And in no sense is meet or amiable.

121 **prisoners** read 'pris'ners.' 129 **five hundred** Lucentio is ex-
aggerating—or has made some side-bets. 130 **laying** betting.
131–2 **Katherine . . . husbands** F sets as prose. 141 **fame** repu-
tation.

A woman mov'd is like a fountain troubled,
Muddy, ill-seeming, thick, bereft of beauty;
And while it is so, none so dry or thirsty   145
Will deign to sip or touch one drop of it.
Thy husband is thy lord, thy life, thy keeper,
Thy head, thy sovereign; one that cares for thee,
And for thy maintenance commits his body
To painful labor both by sea and land,   150
To watch the night in storms, the day in cold,
Whilst thou li'st warm at home, secure and safe;
And craves no other tribute at thy hands
But love, fair looks, and true obedience;
Too little payment for so great a debt.   155
Such duty as the subject owes the prince,
Even such a woman oweth to her husband;
And when she is froward, peevish, sullen, sour,
And not obedient to his honest will,
What is she but a foul contending rebel   160
And graceless traitor to her loving lord?—
I am asham'd that women are so simple
To offer war where they should kneel for peace,
Or seek for rule, supremacy, and sway,
When they are bound to serve, love, and obey.   165
Why are our bodies soft and weak and smooth,
Unapt to toil and trouble in the world,
But that our soft conditions and our hearts
Should well agree with our external parts?
Come, come, you forward and unable worms!   170
My mind hath been as big as one of yours,
My heart as great, my reason haply more,
To bandy word for word and frown for frown;
But now I see our lances are but straws,   174

143 **mov'd** angry. 167 **Unapt** unsuited. 168 **conditions** charac-
teristics.

110

Our strength as weak, our weakness past compare,
That seeming to be most which we indeed least are.
Then vail your stomachs, for it is no boot,
And place your hands below your husband's foot:
In token of which duty, if he please,
My hand is ready; may it do him ease.   180

  Petruchio. Why, there's a wench! Come on and kiss
    me, Kate.

  Lucentio. Well, go thy ways, old lad, for thou shalt
    ha't.

  Vincentio. 'Tis a good hearing when children are
    toward.

  Lucentio. But a harsh hearing when women are fro-
    ward.

  Petruchio. Come, Kate, we'll to bed.   185
We three are married, but you two are sped.
'Twas I won the wager, [*To Lucentio.*] though you
    hit the white;
And, being a winner, God give you good night!
            Exit Petruchio [with Katherina].

  Hortensio. Now, go thy ways; thou hast tam'd a
    curst shrow.   189

  Lucentio. 'Tis a wonder, by your leave, she will be
    tam'd so.   [*Exeunt.*]

FINIS

177 **Then . . . boot** so bring down your pride, for it is of no use.
183 **toward** obedient. 186 **sped** done for. 187 **white** center of the
target, with play on the name Bianca, meaning 'white.'

NOTES

Act I, Scene 1

Act I, Scene 1 Editors, following Pope, have disregarded the Folio and have labeled the first two scenes of the play 'The Induction.' Our text follows the Folio here as well as in the beginnings of Acts IV and V which were altered by Pope and Warburton.

1 Sly A Stephen Sly lived in Stratford in Shakespeare's lifetime, and although the name Slie does appear in *A Shrew*, it is likely that Shakespeare is making use of his native country and its inhabitants. A family by the name of Hacket did live in Wincot, so the reference to Marian Hacket, the fat ale-wife of Wincot (I.2.22–23) enforces this view. There is added interest in the fact that a Will Sly was a member of Shakespeare's company.

9 St. Jeronimy Many editors amend to read 'Go by, Jeronimy,' a phrase from Kyd's *Spanish Tragedy* (III.12.31) and said to be current in Shakespeare's day as an expression of impatience or dismissal. The rest of the line may echo Hieronimo's speech in the same play (II.5.1): 'What outcries pluck me from my naked bed?'

17–18 Broach *Brach* of l. 17 seems clearly an error in the Folio (perhaps the printer's eye strayed to the end of the following line) not only because Merriman is a name commonly given a dog and not a bitch but more cogently because the construction requires a verb. Various emendations have been suggested: *tash* meaning 'to put on a separate leash,' in contrast to the treatment accorded Clowder who is to be 'coupled' (i.e. put on a double leash) with another dog; *bath* (or *bathe*) not inappropriate for an 'embossed' dog, and *broach* meaning to 'bleed,' Dover Wilson's and Kittredge's choice. The possible spelling of this verb, *broch*, would be close to the Folio and would indicate another likely treatment of the distressed animal. It seems on the whole the happiest choice. For a discussion of this passage see the article on hunting by J. W. Fortescue in *Shakespeare's England*, 2, 348–50.

78 Players Bands of strolling players traveled the English countryside presenting their plays wherever they could find an audience, in a market square, a town hall, or in the hall of a nobleman's residence. Particularly in the years 1596–97 when the plague closed the London theatres, Shakespeare's company traveled in the provinces. Hamlet's welcome to the player's (*Hamlet* II.2) indicates the popularity of such groups.

78SD **Enter Players** The stage direction indicates a constant feature of Elizabethan dramatic practice: the necessity for a time interval between an actor's entrance through a door in the back of the stage and his appearance as a speaking character on the forestage. He had to cover a distance of some thirty feet and usually the stage directions indicate entries several lines before the characters speak in order to allow for this. Practically all editors have altered the position of stage directions to suit the proscenium-arch stage, and the Shakespearean playing has thus been lost.

88 **A Player** The Folio's *Sincklo* indicates that this part was played by one Sincklow of the King's company whose name also appears in the Quarto (1600) of *2 Henry IV*, the First Folio version of *3 Henry VI*, and elsewhere, although he does not seem to have been sufficiently important to merit inclusion among the 'Principall Actors' listed at the beginning of the Folio.

88 **Soto** Soto is one of the minor roles in Fletcher's *Woman Pleased* (1620). The reference here is either a later insertion or Fletcher's play goes back to some earlier production of the Shakespearean company.

105 **page** It was the custom of acting companies to employ boys to play the female roles. It was not until the Restoration that the parts were played by women. For an interesting account of a boy actor see Bryher's novel, *The Player's Boy* (New York, 1953).

Act I, Scene 2

50 **Adonis** The story of Adonis, the young hunter beloved of Venus and slain by a wild boar, is retold in Shakespeare's own *Venus and Adonis*.

57 **Daphne** Daphne, a Greek girl loved by Apollo, escaped his pursuit by being turned into the laurel. Lines 57–60 of this scene

suggest Golding's translation of Ovid's *Metamorphoses*, which Shakespeare had read.

93–4 As Stephen Sly . . . Henry Pimpernell Possibly the proper names in these lines are names of real people. There was a Stephen Sly of Stratford, and *Greece* may be a corruption of Greet, a Gloucestershire village, home of 'old John Naps.' See Sydney Lee, *Life of Shakespeare*, p. 167.

Act I, Scene 3

2–3 Padua . . . Lumbardy Padua is a town in northeastern Italy, famous for its University. Lumbardy (Lombardy) is here rather loosely used as a general term for northern Italy. It includes the region modern Italians know as Venetia, where Padua is located.

37 Metaphysics Tranio is here talking about the subjects studied in universities of the time.

47SD Pantaloon This is the name of one of the *maschere* or stock characters in the old Italian *commedia dell' arte*. Traditionally the name was used for the role of an old man, often the butt of other characters. Presumably Gremio is here garbed in the costume of such a character, with slippers, spectacles, and baggy pantaloons. Shakespeare (*As You Like It*, II.7) so describes the sixth of man's seven ages:

> The sixth age shifts
> Into the lean and slipper'd pantaloon
> With spectacles on nose and pouch on side,
> His youthful hose, well saved, a world too wide
> For his shrunk shank; and his big manly voice
> Turning again to childish trebles, pipes
> And whistles in his sound.

55 cart Disorderly women were sometimes punished by being driven around the town in an open cart, exposed to the jeers of the populace.

106–107 Their love is not so great Some editors believe that *their* refers to the love between Katherina and her father (which is not so great as to prevent him from appreciating Bianca); others interpret it as referring to the love between Bianca and Baptista. Dover Wilson, following the Quarto and earlier editors, prints *There, love* . . . Later Folios read *our* for *their*.

152 **love in idleness** This is the popular name of the pansy, here probably used literally; cf. *A Midsummer Night's Dream* II,1.166 ff.

155 **Anna** She was the sister and confidante of Dido, queen of Carthage; cf. *Aeneid*, Bk IV.

163 **Redime . . . minimo** The Latin means 'Ransom your captive self as cheaply as you can.' The phrase quoted (incorrectly) from Terence (*Eunuchus* I.1.29) appears in Lyly's Latin grammar where Shakespeare apparently found it.

169 **daughter of Agenor** Zeus, in the form of a bull, carried off Europa, daughter of Agenor, to Crete; cf. Ovid, *Metamorphoses*, II, 858 ff.

Act I, Scene 4

69 **Florentius** Florentius is the knight who in Gower's version (in the *Confessio Amantis*) of the old fairy tale promised to marry an old hag in return for the solution of a riddle that would save his life. Much against his will he kept his promise, and his bride turned into a beautiful maiden. Chaucer also tells this story in 'The Wife of Bath's Tale.'

70 **Sybil** The Cumean Sybil was granted extreme longevity by Apollo who bestowed on her as many years as the grains of sand which she could hold in her hand.

257 **Alcides** The Pythian oracle at Delphi ordered Hercules to serve Eurystheus, king of Tiryus, for the space of twelve years. During this time he performed twelve feats of extraordinary bravery and strength which are commonly referred to as 'the twelve labors of Hercules.'

Act II, Scene 1

33 **dance barefoot on her wedding day** It was popularly believed that an unmarried elder sister could gain a husband by dancing barefoot at the wedding of her younger sister; thus the phrase is a proverbial description of an old maid.

183–92 Several puns occur in these lines: *hard—heard* (pronounced 'hard'), *bonny—bony* (the F spelling), *Kates—cates* (sweetmeats), and *sounded* 'proclaimed,' with a quibble in the following line on the meaning 'plumbed.'

188 **Kate-Hall** Kate-Hall may refer to St Catherine's Hall at Cambridge or to 'a dining house at Katharine Hall' (New Cambridge ed.) where Queen Elizabeth stopped during a royal progress in 1591.

208 **Ay, for a turtle . . .** Bond reads *she* for *he*, suggesting that the initial letter may have been lost in the final *s* of *as*. He interprets Katherina's speech thus: 'A fool may well think her meek and manageable, as she thinks him' or else, 'as she takes a buzzard for a buzzard,' i.e. a fool for a fool. But it is perhaps better to take *buzzard* in the third sense given above, 'a large insect,' usually a large moth or cockchafer (OED).

288–289 **Grissel . . . Lucrece** Griselda, wife of the Marquis of Saluzzo, in Boccaccio's tale (*Decameron* X, 10) blindly obeyed her husband, and hence became the paragon of wifely docility. Lucrece, a Roman matron who, violated by Sextus, son of King Tarquin of Rome, killed herself, became the symbol of chastity and wifely honor. Cf. Shakespeare's *The Rape of Lucrece.*

Act III, Scene 1

4 **know this lady's** Hamner first suggested this emendation which clarifies the meaning and gives the line its proper number of syllables.

28–9 **Hic ibat . . . celsa senis** 'Here flowed Simois; here is the Trojan land; here stood old Priam's lofty palace.' Ovid, *Heroides* I. 33–4.

37–39 This is the F arrangement. Some editors, however, reproduce these lines as verse, thus:

> *Hortensio.* Madam, my instrument's in tune.
> *Bianca.*   Let's hear.
> O fie! the treble jars.
> *Lucentio.*   Spit in the hole, man,
> And tune again.

46–49 F assigns these lines to Lucentio.

50–51 F assigns these lines to Bianca.

52–56 F assigns these lines to Hortensio.

65 **gamouth** *Gamouth* is the Elizabethan spelling of *gamut*, the name for the diatonic scale. This derives from the Greek *gamma* which was the name of the first note in the scale. The suffix *-ut*

denotes the first note of a hexachord and the resultant word acquires the meaning of all the notes in the scale.

80 **Messenger** The Folio *Nicke* may quite possibly refer to Nicholas Tooley, listed among the 'Principall actors of all these plays' in the First Folio. This hardly seems a part for a 'principal actor' but we may assume he played other parts as well.

Act III, Scene 2

30 **old** The reference to *old* in the following line suggests that its omission in this one is an error. Many editors (following Capell) amend to read: 'news, old news, and such news.' We are inclined to agree with Dover Wilson that the insertion of the word after *such* seems 'the simplest and most natural' reading.

67–68 **humor of forty fancies** Doubtless Dover Wilson is right in his assertion that 'no one knows what this phrase means.' Our note follows Halliwell; other guesses include 'some ballad or drollery' (Warburton), 'a collection of short poems such as were called fancies' (Steevens), 'a fantastic ornament comprising the humor of forty different fancies' (Malone).

Act III, Scene 3

Scene 3 Pope, disregarding the act division indicated in the Folio text, chose to begin the fourth act at this point. All subsequent editors have followed this arbitrary emendation. The present text follows the Folio.

85 **indifferent knit.** The ambiguous word is *indifferent*, variously explained as 'not different' (Johnson), 'particolor' (Malone) and with adverbial meaning (Bond) as we have taken it.

135 **Food . . . food** The Folio *soud* has baffled the commentators. Some have taken it as an indication of a sound expressing fatigue, some see in it an echo of the refrain of an old song, 'Soudledum, soudledum' (Halliwell) and Hammer took it as representing the humming of Petruchio. Dover Wilson's emendation *Food*, which we have followed, certainly seems appropriate to the circumstances and the stage business, and is understandable as a printer's confusion of long *s* and *f*.

185 **lure** A lure was a small wicker container covered with

feathers used first in training a hawk. Meat was placed inside and the falconer swung the lure in a circle over his head to create a whistling sound. The hawk pouncing on the lure received her food. After the hawk was trained, the mere swinging up of the lure would recall her.

190 **Last night . . . shall not** Either this is a guess on Petruchio's part or Shakespeare has forgotten that the pair has been married only today.

201 **kill a wife with kindness** Of this line Bond wisely remarks: 'This being a common phrase for mistaken indulgence, we need not suppose an allusion to Heywood's *A Woman Killed with Kindness*, 1607, nor adjust the date of our play thereto.'

Act III, Scene 4

8–11 **Art of Love** An allusion to Ovid's *Ars amatoria*. These lines contain a series of common puns, namely *art—heart—hart* (pronounced alike), *dear—deer*, and *proceeders*, with a play on its usual meaning and the sense of candidates for degree, with reference to the master of art of l. 9.

57 **tricks eleven and twenty long** This is an allusion to the card game referred to in I, 4, 33, and means 'tricks suitable to the needs of the case.'

Act IV, Scene 2

18SD **Enter Baptista and Lucentio** Since the Pedant is already on the stage, the stage direction in the Folio is either an afterthought or an instruction to the Pedant to remove his hat at the entrance of Baptista and Lucentio. Such directions for stage business are rather rare in the Folio.

67–8 **I pray . . . my heart** The Folio's assignment of l. 67 to Biondello has caused some editors to change the *Cambio* of l. 62 to *Biondello*. Yet here Perry's reasoning (Yale Shakespeare, 1928) is quite convincing: Lucentio is Baptista's servant and so would naturally be ordered about by him; furthermore it is essential to the plot to have Bianca fetched by Lucentio. We may assume that Lucentio moves off to another part of the stage, where he awaits Biondello. The Folio provides only one *Exit* but the stage direction of l. 72 seems to indicate that the pair has joined up, either on stage as indicated or just off stage. I would take it that Tranio's speech in l. 68, though picking up Lucentio's phrase, is addressed to Biondello in dismissal. The Folio SD of l. 68 has baffled editors; Bond suggests Peter may be the name of an actor, playing the part of a servant come to tell Tranio that dinner awaits.

93 **cum . . . solem** This is an ancient copyright formula meaning 'with privilege of exclusive printing' (*cum privilegio ad imprimendum solum*); it is here used metaphorically by Biondello, whose Latin is not perfect. Cf. the same metaphorical use of *appendix* in l. 104.

Act IV, Scene 3

25 **bias** In lawn bowling the balls employed are weighted on one side so that they will roll in an arc thus enabling a bowler to go around a ball of an opponent which lies between him and the jack or small white ball which is the target. If the ball is properly bowled it will run *with* and not *against* the bias.

Act IV, Scene 4

Scene 4 Again our text follows the Folio. Warburton began Act V at this point, and all subsequent editors have followed him rather than the Folio.

46 **I . . . sir** This expression was used to a disagreeable person who barred one's path in the street, according to the New Cambridge editors; cf. *The Merchant of Venice*, I.2.45.

APPENDIX A

Text and Date

The text of this edition follows that of the First Folio (1623), the earliest printed version of the play. The First Quarto edition (1631) is based on the First Folio as are the versions of all subsequent Folio editions (of which there are three).

We have had before us the facsimile edition of the First Folio (Oxford, 1902) and have made our basic principle fidelity to the text. We have, however, indicated some act and scene divisions missing in the Folio and supplied a few stage directions which have become conventional. We have also modernized the spelling, except in cases where the spelling reveals the pronunciation of the time, and we have repunctuated in line with modern practice. Apart from such changes all departures from the Folio reading, for the most part of very minor nature, are indicated in the glosses or notes.

APPENDIX B

Sources

In discussing the sources of *The Taming of the Shrew* one must bear in mind that as the play stands it contains three plot ingredients: the beggar transported to a higher realm, the wife tamed, and a pair of lovers united by the machinations of quick-witted servants. All of these elements are of considerable antiquity. The beggar motif goes back as far at least as the *Arabian Nights*. The theme of shrew-taming, in the words of Sir Arthur Quiller-Couch, is 'as old as the hills,' though we may note that it is also the subject of several folk ballads closer to Shakespeare's own time, for example, *A Merry Jest of a Shrewd and Curst Wife Lapped in Morel's Skin for her Good Behavior* (mid-16th century). The devices of the subplot go back through Ariosto to Roman comedy.

The remote sources are clear enough in the main. When we touch on the question of Shakespeare's immediate source we enter more dangerous ground—not by any means unsurveyed but rather too carefully and contradictorily charted. For we must begin with an examination of the relationship of our play to the earlier work *The Taming of a Shrew* (referred to for brevity as *A Shrew*), a problem that has teased Shakespearean editors and critics over the years and which still awaits a solution satisfactory to all. While the first printed edition of *The Shrew* appears in the First Folio (1623), *A Shrew* was published in 1594, and Henslowe's Diary notes, for June of that same year, a performance of a play of that name by the Lord Chamberlain's servants (i.e. Shakespeare's company) at Newington Butts. *A Shrew* is made of coarser stuff than *The Shrew;* it is by comparison of unpolished texture, and the characterization is cruder; indeed it is by nature a farce. At the same time it is in certain respects a more finished product than *The Shrew:* Sly is not ignored after the introductory scenes but consistent use is made of him for comment and at the end he goes off content with the moral of wife-beating, and—another example of tidiness—Katherina is provided with a second sister who pairs off with Hortensio.

The similarities, however, are much more noteworthy than the differences. Both plays begin with the prank played on Sly; the main plot follows an identical development with many scenes the same in action and often in wording; the subplot, borrowed from Gascoigne's *The Supposes* (1556), a translation of Ludovico Ariosto's *I Suppositi* (1509), is likewise similar, though here some minor differences may be noted. The role of Tranio, the elderly suitor (Gremio), the Pedant's relationship to the disguised servant, the device used to persuade the Pedant to undertake his imposture, the confronting of the true and false fathers, the names Petruchio and Licio (though assigned to minor characters in Gascoigne's play)—all these are elements found in both *The Supposes* and the subplot of *The Shrew* though not in *A Shrew*. It seems clear that Shakespeare was not content, as far as the secondary plot was concerned, to take the material from *A Shrew* but went back to Gascoigne whose play thus becomes doubly, at first and second hand as it were, the source of the subplot of *The Shrew*.

Yet this is merely to lay the groundwork for the main problem of the relationship between *A Shrew* and *The Shrew*. Given the priority of printing dates and Henslowe's reference, the normal assumption would be that *A Shrew* is the older play and Shakespeare, in accordance with the habits of the times and indeed his own practice, used it as a basis for his own creation. This is in fact a perfectly tenable theory. But there are others. One, advanced relatively recently by P. Alexander (in the *Time Literary Supplement*, Sept. 16, 1926), holds that the printed version of *A Shrew* is a memorial reconstruction (i.e. a version taken down from the memorization of actors) of the play that we know as *The Shrew*, explaining the differences above noted as adaptations deemed necessary for the presentation before provincial audiences. According to this theory Henslowe actually saw *The Shrew*. This theory has convinced one of the editors of the New Cambridge edition of the play, Dover Wilson, though not his colleague, Quiller-Couch.

Yet a third hypothesis, advanced by Ten Brink (in the *Shakespeare-Jahrbuch, 12* [1877], 94), suggests that both plays go back to the common source of an original Shrew play, *eine*

Jugendarbeit Shakespeares in Ten Brink's opinion. The most recent advocate of the Ten Brink theory is Hardin Craig who, without attributing the source to Shakespeare's own hand, postulates 'a lost original shrew play.' Craig argues that such a hypothesis not only would explain the discrepancies in the plays but also 'has the advantage of showing that everybody is right and everybody is wrong. That is, *A Shrew* might readily be mistaken for the source of *The Shrew*, because *A Shrew* is a version of that source. It might readily be regarded as a "bad" quarto of *The Shrew*, because it is a "bad" quarto of the source of *The Shrew*.' [1]

Those who argue for the memorial reconstruction theory are at least spared the burden of finding a suitable author for the early play, save of course insofar as they may regard both works as collaborative enterprises. Critics who cannot accept *A Shrew* as Shakespeare's work have so far failed to reach unanimous accord on any one author; it has been assigned, in the words of Bond 'in turn to every near and important predecessor of Shakespeare save Lyly and Nash'; many modern critics have seen in it the hand of some imitator of Marlowe, and Quiller-Couch indeed finds 'nothing incredible' in the supposition that Marlowe may have written it himself 'with or without collaborators.' Pope, without waiting for the theory of memorial reconstruction, claimed *A Shrew* for Shakespeare himself, a claim recently restated by Courthope in his *History of English Poetry*.

As for the authorship of *The Shrew*, although various editors have sensed the presence of another hand than Shakespeare's, especially in the subplot, opinion has been by no means unanimous on this point and most recently editions, though hesitantly, and with various shades of reservation, attribute the work to Shakespeare. Bond, for example, after enumerating the scenes that have by common consent been assigned to Shakespeare adds for the rest, 'while admitting the presence of other work, I do not feel that we have ground enough for denying Shakespeare's re-

1 '*The Shrew* and *A Shrew;* Possible Settlement of an Old Debate,' in *Elizabethan Studies and Other Essays in Honor of George F. Reynolds*, Boulder, 1945, p. 154.

vision, however hasty, of the whole.' Quiller-Couch, too, seems reluctant to accept a collaborator; for his colleague, Dover Wilson, Shakespeare either 'created or recreated the play,' and Craig in his recent edition of Shakespeare's plays (New York, 1952) also thinks of it as 'probably' Shakespeare's play.

There can be no general agreement on the date of the play, in view of the various theories of its relationship to *A Shrew*. Some rather complicated reasoning by Bond leads him to date the play as of 1594–95, Craig opts for 1593, and Dover Wilson would place it 'before the summer of 1592 or at any rate before 2 May 1594.' [2]

2 For further discussion of the genesis of *The Shrew*, in addition to the authorities cited, see: R. A. Houk, 'Evolution of *The Taming of the Shrew*,' PMLA, December 1942, pp. 1009–38; and 'Strata in the *Taming of the Shrew*,' *Studies in Philology*, 1942, 291–302; H. Dugdale Sykes, *The Authorship of 'The Taming of a Shrew*,' Shakespeare Association, 1919; E. P. Kuhl, 'The Authorship of *The Taming of the Shrew*,' PMLA, *40*, 551–618; G. I. Duthie, '*The Taming of a Shrew* and *The Taming of the Shrew*' (*Review of English Studies*, *19* (1948), 337–56).

APPENDIX C
Reading List

Frederick S. Boas, *Shakespeare and His Predecessors*, 1896, pp. 172–81.

R. Warwick Bond, ed., *The Taming of the Shrew*, *The Arden Shakespeare*, London, 1904.

Henry B. Charlton, *Shakespearian Comedy*, 4th ed., London, 1949, pp. 73–99.

William Hazlitt, *Characters of Shakespeare's Plays*, 1817, pp. 312–20.

Thomas Marc Parrott, *Shakespearean Comedy*, New York, 1949, pp. 144–53.

Sir Arthur Quiller-Couch and John Dover Wilson, eds., *The Taming of the Shrew*, The New Cambridge Shakespeare, Cambridge, 1928.